BLISS
AND
TRAGEDY

The Ashtabula Railway-Bridge Accident
of 1876 and the Loss of P. P. Bliss

BLISS  TRAGEDY

The Ashtabula Railway-Bridge Accident
of 1876 and the Loss of P. P. Bliss

Edited by
THOMAS E. CORTS

Ashtabula County Historical Society
Ashtabula, Ohio

Bliss and Tragedy

ISBN-13: 978-1-931985-09-3
ISBN-10: 1-931985-09-X

Published by Samford University Press

Samford University Press
Samford University
800 Lakeshore Drive
Birmingham, Alabama 35229 U.S.A.
www.samford.edu

Editor: Thomas E. Corts
Assistant Editor: Sandra L. O'Brien
Cover Designer: Scott E. Camp

Printed in the United States of America
17   16   15   3   4   5   6

To the memories of my mother and father
Hazel Louise Vernon Corts (1912–1998)
Charles Harold Corts (1912–1998)
who gave me the advantage of
an Ashtabula boyhood
and
To the memories of my mother-in-law and father-in-law
Ruth Johnson Haas (1913–2000)
Herman Amazon Haas (1908–1995)
who gave me my lifelong best friend.

Table of Contents

Preface 2008

The public has been kind to embrace *Bliss and Tragedy: The Ashtabula Railway-Bridge Accident of 1876 and the Loss of P. P. Bliss.* Most readers have commented that the book clarified long-standing misconceptions. Proceeds from the sale of the book have benefited the Jennie Munger Gregory Memorial Museum at Geneva-on-the-Lake, Ohio, a project of the Ashtabula County Historical Society. The Society and its members have been excellent stewards of the revenue, using the proceeds to enhance the collection, its accessibility and usefulness. A special debt of thanks is owed Jean Metcalf, truly a "book-keeper," a volunteer, who flawlessly consigned the books and accounted for the income. Jean also made maintenance of the museum a high priority, donating thousands of hours of time and good common sense to the careful preservation and organization of materials. Barbara Hamilton, with Jean Metcalf, first called my attention to the long misplaced/overlooked trove of articles and artifacts related to the disaster. As the unofficial historian of Ashtabula County, she never wearies of telling the Ashtabula story.

My debt to the authors included here is still very real. All our life circumstances have changed with the times, but it pleases us that our work is still deemed useful and worthy of reprinting.

The Reverend Virgil Reeve and his wife, Evelyn, transplants to Ashtabula, now retired elsewhere, early saw the impact of the horrific tragedy on the town of Ashtabula, and the sad loss of the Blisses. The Reverend Reeve was relentless in arranging every detail for the commemorative event of 2002, marking the tragedy and the loss of Philip Paul and Lucy Young Bliss. He was equally enthusiastic about the historical marker, the kiosk, and the book. His photographs are his obvious contribution to the volume; less observable was his tracking down facts, scanning articles and data, and serving as an indefatigable cheerleader. Though now retired and moved away, the Reeve's cords of personal friendship, just as their ties to Ashtabula, remain unbroken.

The most satisfying aspect of studying a historical figure up close and personal is to sense when the study is done that the individual is worthy. Philip Paul and Lucy Young Bliss were persons of sterling Christian character, deeply caring for others, selflessly disinterested in material wealth and possessions. Their legacy, as examples of persons devoted to the Lord and His children, is every bit as profound as their bequest of music that still stirs the soul after more than 125 years.

It was very satisfying to dedicate this book to the memories of my dear parents and my dear parents-in-law. The Lord's gracious Providence has overflowed my cup, affording me dedicated parents, loving siblings, the exactly right spouse, significant work, a lifetime of dear friends, treasured children, beautiful grandchildren—and, overflowing the overflow, allowing me, even in mature years, to come close to P. P. and Lucy Bliss.

Thomas E. Corts
Birmingham, Alabama
May 2008

Introduction

This volume owes its existence to The Reverend Virgil V. Reeve. He came to prominence in Ashtabula when he came to pastor First Baptist Church. In February of 2002, we introduced ourselves to one another by e-mail. I lamented the city's slight notice of the 125th anniversary of the Ashtabula train-bridge disaster that had claimed the lives of songwriter Philip Paul Bliss and his wife, along with many others. He had been aware of the anniversary, but said it was a good thing no commemorative event had been planned, since December 29, 2001, the anniversary date, had spawned a blizzard almost as difficult as that of December 29, 1876, closing churches, businesses, and bringing the city to a slow crawl.

So, hastily he went to work and assembled a planning committee of local ministers and supporters. On August 1–3, 2002, we held "Bliss and Tragedy: A 125th Year Remembrance of Songwriter Philip Paul Bliss and the Ashtabula Bridge Disaster." Many people had a hand in helping with the event, which also resulted in establishment of a kiosk at Ashtabula County Medical Center, and an historical marker. Preparing for presentations at the symposium, we realized that authors had uncovered information about the people and the disaster that had long been hidden. It seemed a worthy contribution to review all that we know about the train wreck, a defining moment in the city's history, and compile it in one accessible volume—the first such book devoted to the disaster since 1877.

This volume is partial repayment toward a great debt I owe Ashtabula, this city of my growing up. I walked these streets to deliver the *Ashtabula Star Beacon* and the *Cleveland Plain Dealer,* played on the banks of the gulf, washed cars at the Jack W. Ross Funeral Home, attended Daily Vacation Bible School at First Baptist Church, bought clothes at Schaeffer's Dry Goods Store (when I would have preferred to buy them at Carlisle–Allen), clerked at Bill Graham's Delicatessen, learned to drive on county roads in order to take the dreaded driver's test (three times) at Jefferson, and married the girl whose hand I held in the Junior Class Play. In the public schools from grades 3–12, I remember remarkably competent teachers, my Ashtabula education crowned by membership in the most unusual Ashtabula High School Class of 1959, whose blessed ties still bind.

Though now living in New Jersey, Florida, North Carolina, Arizona, Alabama, and the District of Columbia, my siblings and I hold Ashtabula in fond memory. In 1948, my father purchased the

Ashtabula Business College, which he operated with sporadic but never great success, gradually phasing it out in the mid-'80s. He was an ordained minister and nearly always had a part-time church in the rural areas east of Ashtabula or in western Pennsylvania. There were seven children in the family, and all, save one, were graduated from Ashtabula High School:

> Naomi Ruth Corts White, '51
> John Ronald Corts, '53
> Charles Mark Corts, '55
> David Livingstone Corts, '57
> Thomas Edward Corts, '59
> Paul Richard Corts, '61.

Our youngest brother, Philip Chris Corts, who died in 1997, was graduated from Cochranton (Pennsylvania) High School, Class of '68.

All that makes your hometown home, even after you have seen the world, is in my heart and mind. Memory is often a better playground than reality, but the reality, as I recall it, requires no enhancement.

Many people have had a strong hand in this project. Each of the writers has been interested from the very first in assuring accuracy of facts and telling the human side of the story. From our initial meetings via e-mail, we have felt a certain loyalty and common commitment to perpetuating the story of the Ashtabula bridge disaster. The Steering Committee for the event in the summer of 2002, took its task very seriously. (See Appendix F.) Folks at the Ashtabula Public Library, where I took my little brother for story time five decades ago, were understanding to let us use the resources of the Ohio Room. Jean Metcalf was devoted to the Jennie Munger Gregory Memorial Museum at Geneva-on-the-Lake. She not only gained us access to the museum's pertinent holdings, but actually worked on this project like a longtime friend. Kathleen Lehto at Hubbard House–Underground Railroad Museum gave of her time to share information about mementos there.

Anyone interested in Ashtabula's great tragedy of 1876 has to honor the memory of The Reverend Stephen D. Peet, author of *The Ashtabula Disaster* (1877). One-time pastor of Ashtabula's Congregational Church, with a pastor's heart and a historian's awareness, he conducted extensive interviews of persons surviving the wreck, and chronicled the first and only book on the event, though more compassionate than accurate.

For a person with my values and convictions, I probably am

blessed to have the finest job in the world. I serve at the pleasure of the trustees of Samford University, who have been gracious to understand and support my myriad interests. Sandra O'Brien, my assistant, is an experienced editor whose handiwork benefits every reader, though her considerable contribution to this volume is most apparent to me. Becca Williamson is always willing to go the extra mile to increase my efficiency and accommodate my various involvements. Janica York, Scott Camp, and Jack Brymer have brought this volume to completion with a professionalism I appreciate.

The historical account of persons and events of the past should help us to live more meaningfully in the present. In the lives of P. P. and Lucy Bliss, and of many heroes and heroines mentioned in this volume, we could have no finer examples.

Thomas E. Corts

Almost the Perfect Disaster
Darrell E. Hamilton

As chairman of the Ashtabula–Ohio Bicentennial Committee and author of articles in the *Star Beacon,* Darrell Hamilton inspired the Ashtabula community's interest in its distinctive history. This essay is drawn from research Darrell did for his *Star Beacon* series, which relied upon Peet's book, *The Ashtabula Disaster,* as well as contemporary newspapers and private letters of Norris Simons, ticket agent for the railroad on duty the night of the accident.

A little more than 125 years ago, on a bitter cold, stormy night in Ashtabula, a forty-mile-an-hour gale was blowing, three feet of snow were on the ground, and the temperature hovered around sixteen degrees. In many places, the strong wind had thrown huge drifts of snow six feet or higher.

Running east and west through the Village of Ashtabula was the Lake Shore Railway, dividing about 2500 residents, several small places of business, three saloons, and three hotels. A defining characteristic of the village topography was "the gulf," described by some as the "deep gorge," as deep as 70 to 125 feet in places, and running at least six or seven miles through and beyond the community. The gulf presented a challenge to railroading, and in 1865 the railway opened an experimental iron bridge, replacing an earlier wooden span. There was no road down to the floor of the gulf, where coursed the Ashtabula River, sometimes called Ashtabula "Creek." The only access was a steep set of steps. From the bottom of the gorge, two lofty arcs of stone seventy-six feet high were built, one at each end, nearly 150 feet apart, to anchor the span. Flanking these pillars were smaller abutments of an older bridge left standing, but not used since the new experimental bridge was opened for train traffic. The span of the bridge across the gulf, from abutment to abutment, was the unusual length of 150 feet.

Most people of Ashtabula at the time thought the bridge a scary sight. It was not built as an arch, nor was it supported by abutments below. It was a spidery web of wrought iron, iron-braced, and bolted. There was trouble building the bridge from beginning to end. The engineer who drafted the original plans noted that braces, smaller than intended, were used. The engineer differed so with management over details of construction that he resigned his position. The bridge, however, was built anyway and was still standing eleven years later.

Winter of 1876–77 had already produced three heavy snows. Snow had been falling all day on December 29 and was coming down with blinding fury in very cold temperatures. The gulf's steep steps had disappeared in the snow, businesses had closed early, and travel of any type was difficult. Residents of Ashtabula were inside, snuggled up to warm fireplaces. No one was away from home unless one had to be. One of those having to be away from his home was Norris Simons, the railroad ticket agent, who was on duty at the West 32nd Street depot. (Simons was the great-great-great uncle of the author's wife.)

Another resident out that night was Edward W. Lockwood, who lived on the east side of the gulf and used the bridge to get home. He had crossed the bridge many times, since he could always hear the train's whistle blowing in the distance. This night, however, with the wind and the storm, was destined to be different. Edward had just crossed when he saw the train's oncoming headlight. He hurriedly jumped from the tracks into a snow drift as No. 5 went by. The engineer remembered seeing Lockwood jump from the tracks and looked down on him. It was not quite 7:30 p.m.

Earlier, a train had routinely passed over the bridge, the engineer having noticed a "rumble," but because of the blinding snowstorm and wind, he had paid little attention to it. The No. 5, Pacific Express, had left New York the night before, divided at Albany, a portion of it plunging through snowdrifts in the mountains of Vermont, while the other portion was boring through snow near the banks of Lake Erie. The latter train was due in Erie, Pennsylvania a little after noon, though it was two-and-a-half hours late and should have reached Ashtabula by 5:15 in the evening. Snow was the bane of both parts. Two extra engines, a total of four, had been required to push the western train through accumulated snow at the Erie station. Ironically, both halves of the train were destined to be wrecked, except that the Chicago-bound train would take with it a terrible toll in human lives.

The many accounts of the train wreck at Ashtabula only demonstrate confusion about the number of passengers. Some have stated that the train was filled to capacity, while others observed that many seats were vacant. It seems likely that the snowstorm would have kept many people at home, and there had already been three harsh snowstorms during the month of December. While the train had a capacity of four hundred or more, less than two hundred passengers and nineteen employees were on board at the time. (The exact number was never definitely declared.) The count by railroad officials at the time was 197 passengers, but the number of tickets the conductor had in his possession may have numbered as many as three hundred. Not in the official count were a few who had railroad passes.

The train consisted of two locomotives and their tenders; two express cars; two baggage cars; two day-passenger coaches; a smoking car; a drawing-room car; three sleeper cars. It was a beautiful train and well known for its elegance in an age when railways were fast becoming a glamorous way to travel.

Right before the disaster, ladies in the sleeping coaches were preparing to retire: some had already lain down in their berths. Gentlemen were quietly dozing in their seats, while others were taking their last smoke before settling in for the night. Men were playing cards. Children were already in their berths, some probably already asleep, dreaming of just-completed Christmas visits with grandparents.

Transcontinental passengers, heading to California, mingled with others readying to get off the train in Ashtabula. With the storm raging and the wind blowing, the train must have lent a great sense of security against the intense weather.

Approaching the bridge, the train had begun to slow down, the depot only a hundred yards on the other side of the bridge. The second engine had already started to apply its brakes. Suddenly, the lull of the wheels rolling on the tracks ceased. The bell rope snapped, and lamps went out. In an instant, passengers felt themselves falling, seized by silence as the crack of metal, the breaking of wood rent the snowy stillness, resounding inside the cabins. Breathless, bracing, and seizing the seats before them, passengers spoke not a word, as they awaited their fate and the whereabouts of their unplanned destination.

The engineer of the first engine, Dan McGuire, heard a sharp crack and, looking back, saw the second engine, Columbia, start to sink. With great presence of mind, he opened the throttle all the way to drive his engine forward. With his quick thinking, the first engine, Socrates, reached the firm foundation of the western abutment. The Columbia was drawn forward and almost made it but struck the abutment, and for an instant, clung to the first engine by the coupling rod. In a split second, the coupling broke, and the engine disappeared into the deep, dark gorge below—a gorge commonly serene in the snowy evening, quiet, suddenly invaded by metal shrapnel and human carnage, and desperate people crying out for help, gasping to hold onto life.

The bridge actually broke in the center. While the engine Columbia hung for a second to the first engine, it gave time for the other cars to drop to the gulf floor first. The first car to land was the express car that was behind the second locomotive. It also hit the abutment on its way to the bottom. Unfortunately, for any survivors in the express car, the Columbia fell on top of it instantly killing any who may have survived the fall. The locomotive completely reversed direction, its headlights pointing toward the very cars it had been pulling. The trailing cars then littered the landscape, some having collided with others, some having flown through the air and having landed as much as eighty feet from the sides of the bridge.

Of the passengers to die, some were killed instantly. At first disoriented, survivors crawled through broken windows and debris, in some instances causing worse injury to themselves than they received in the fall. Escaping passengers could hardly see where they were going. They had to feel their way to safety. Some fell through the ice and drowned.

Stoves used to heat passenger cars were by government regulations to be self-extinguishing, though the Pacific Express's that night were not. Later, the railroad was found at fault for the violation. The crash sent fire racing in all directions, breaking through the wreckage and lighting up the valley.

At the depot, railroad employees went outside upon hearing the train's whistle. Knowing the train was more than two hours late made onlookers anxious. Standing on the platform they saw the first locomotive's light approaching. Then, they saw the rest of the train fall behind it. People who lived near the depot heard the sounds of cars falling in quick succession.

First to descend the steps of the gulf were railroad employees and a saloon keeper from one nearby hotel. Most ignored the snowy steps and slid down the incline to the wreck site instantly, appalled at the destruction. They followed instinct and immediately chopped through wreckage with axes to free survivors and to get them up the gulf-side to help.

Meanwhile, flames began to rise, from what was at first only a glimmering light. Fire began at each end of the wreck and came together, west to east, in a powerful bonfire. The few people on the scene were getting the trapped out of the wreckage.

Simultaneously, the fire department, under the control of an alcoholic fire chief, slow in mind and body, and unfit for the job, seemed paralyzed. When firemen reached the scene with a steamer and hoses, no orders were given to fight the fire. The fire chief was heard to say that there was no use in throwing water on the flames. It was common understanding that railroad policy was to let any on-fire train burn. That policy had never given consideration to the possibility that people might be on board. While the fire chief could have ordered the fire to be put out, he was confused, immobilized, and unable to take control. Even as firemen laid out hose to the pumper, he never brought himself to give the simple order. A hand pumper and a steam pumper stood by idly while the fire intensified. Someone ran up from the wreck begging, "For God's sake, water should be thrown," but no orders were given, even as people below called out for buckets. Finally, buckets were procured, and water was thrown on the flames, well-intentioned volunteers doing what firemen would not, though their efforts were too late. The flames were out of control.

With fire growing more intense and sweeping the entire site, many were still trapped. One man was pressed beneath the locomotive and burned to death as rescuers tried to lift the locomotive from his legs. A lady screamed as her dress caught fire, but no one could reach her.

A father was able to get his children to safety and then went back for his wife, who was clamped beneath the weight of the wreckage. Unable to be freed, hearing other passengers screaming as they burned to death, she pleaded with her husband to slit her throat before the flames overtook her. In desperation, he was able to get help, and she was saved.

Flames became so intense that buckets of water were futile. Screams of agony could be heard by nearby residents as victims perished, trapped inside the railcars. It was a night the people of Ashtabula would never forget.

The famous Christian songwriter Philip Paul Bliss was also on board the train that fateful night. Earlier that evening, he had been seen working, probably on his latest composition. Some accounts claim that Bliss fought in vain to save his wife and children, all to no avail. Bliss's children were not on board, and the story is doubtful.

The last survivor pulled from the wreckage was a dog, a bull terrier that had been tied in the baggage car. The injured and dying were carried up the steep snow-covered steps, or pulled up on sleigh or sled by a brigade of volunteers to the engine house, first, then elsewhere. The nearest structure, other than the engine house, located on the bank, was the Eagle Hotel. The first eleven injured were sheltered there, unluckily. The Hotel was a horrid place, even by standards of that day, with a dirty barroom, tiny guest rooms without stoves, rooms that had never been carpeted with space just large enough for a bed and washstand. Beds were miserable straw ticks with filthy sheets.

Passengers rescued subsequently were taken to better hotels. When the supply of rooms was exhausted, the injured were laid on couches in the lobbies, counters of stores, and the truly fortunate found solace in private homes. Others ended up in the Ashtabula House still standing at the corner of West 46th Street and Main Avenue. The injured who could walk—among the last to be brought up—were tied to a sleigh and pulled up the side of the banks.

Before midnight, all survivors had been brought up from the gulf. By 1:00 a.m., railroad officials arrived by train from Cleveland with five surgeons. Ten village doctors and surgeons worked all night on the injured. Repairing broken limbs and performing amputations were not uncommon. Among the severely injured were the engineer and fireman, who, surprisingly, survived the fall to the bottom of the gulf in the Columbia. The fireman Peter Livenbroe of Cleveland died January 3, 1877, apparently of congestion of the lungs (*Ashtabula Sentinel*, January 4, 1877).

With all survivors rescued, no living soul was about the unguarded crash site. Crimes of thievery had actually begun earlier in the evening. A young man, who had just lost both mother and sister, was suffering from four broken ribs and a severe gash to the head. As he looked up and saw men standing on the banks watching him, the thought of robbery crossed his mind. He had a valuable watch, a present from his father, and two money purses, one with fifty dollars and the other, with a few dollars in change. He also carried his dead mother's jewelry. As he thought of thieves, he turned with his back to the group and dropped his watch inside his shirt. One money purse he placed in an inside vest pocket and the other remained in the pocket of his pantaloons. His mother's jewelry was carefully placed inside his undergarments.

He had been assisted up the gulf by a kindly helper, doing his best for the injured and dying. Atop the bank, he was handed over to another, who walked him only a short distance in the darkness before dealing the boy a body blow. The pain was so intense that he passed out and was left lying in the snow. When he regained consciousness, he had been robbed of almost everything including his train ticket to California. His mother's jewelry, though concealed, was gone. The only thing the thieves overlooked was his gold pocket watch he had dropped inside his shirt. Others helped him to a hotel where he had the sad duty to telegraph his father in California the horrible news of his mother's and sister's deaths.

Other survivors told of being robbed in similar manner. The conscious and unconscious alike had been preyed upon. One man, with a huge splinter of wood, a damaged fragment of the railcar he was riding in, driven through his shoulder, was robbed of three hundred dollars, while he laid in the Eagle Hotel. The boots of another man were taken off and spirited away while he lay unconscious. Anyone wearing an article of clothing of apparent value was subject to thievery. Some thieves actually wore black masks to hide their identities. Even trunks were hauled off: trunks containing the wardrobe of a new bride and those belonging to survivors whose permanent homes were in the village.

Most burned bodies were not identified. Had thieves not robbed the jewelry and belongings, chances are they would have been identified and not buried in Chestnut Grove Cemetery among "the unrecognized dead."

The fire and the thieves worked their plunder, while the doctors worked all night trying to save survivors. The sheer horror and magnitude of the event, the significant loss of life, they were not fully realized in the dark, in the race of adrenalin that had charged the night of the accident. Everyone, including those at the scene the night before, was about to learn that they had witnessed the single worst bridge disaster in United States history.

One person who worked all night to help survivors was Fred W. Blakeslee, a member of the Ashtabula Volunteer Fire Department. Though the fire company never worked to put out the fire, a call had gone out to department members of Ashtabula, and many survivors were rescued by firemen. Blakeslee, just twenty-one years old, had recently opened a photographic studio in Ashtabula with his partner, Mr. Moore, on Main Avenue at the site of the present Masonic Temple building.

After midnight, when the fire burned down and all the living had been rescued, Blakeslee had gone home to rest. Sensing the opportunity to document the event, Saturday morning he got his horse and sleigh, loaded his bulky camera, plates, and sensitizing materials, essential for the crude photography of the time, and went back to the site. Clambering down the icy steps with his cumbersome camera and equipment to the pumping station just west of the bridge, he set up and attempted to record the event for history. Because of the bitter cold, photographic solutions kept freezing. He had to warm his plates and photographic solutions inside a switchman's shanty to keep them from freezing when he stepped back out into the cold.

The *Ashtabula News,* following the custom of all newspapers of that day, blurring the lines between paid advertisements and news, carried a paragraph in its January 3, 1877 issue, under "Local Brevities."

anyway. During the bridge's erection, the engineer, Mr. Joseph Tomlinson, differed so strongly with the president that he resigned his position. The thought of resignation had also passed through Charles Collins' mind, as he said later.

Charles Collins had worked that fateful night in freezing water, higher than his waist, hoping to save people in the wreckage. He saw firsthand the destruction, death, and mangled bodies of men, women, and children. An employee of the railroad for thirty years, Collins was widely respected among fellow railroad employees and in the community.

Days after the disaster, in a weakened state of mind, he had wept in front of the press. Family and friends became concerned about him. A gentle, sensitive man, he was filled with emotion over the disaster and fell into momentary outbursts of grief. On New Year's Day 1877, at his wife's parents' house on the east side of Ashtabula, he had stepped outside to get some fresh air before breakfast. A coachman, passing by the house, wished Charles a Happy New Year, and he returned the greeting. As he sat down at the breakfast table, he burst into tears and covered his face with his hands, sobbing to his wife, "John bid me a Happy New Year this morning, but how can it be a happy New Year to me?"

As his stability of mind seemed to worsen, Collins tendered his resignation from the railroad. With tears in his eyes he said, "I have worked for thirty years with what fidelity God knows, for the protection and safety of the public, and now the public, forgetting all these years of service, has turned against me." The resignation was not accepted, and Collins was assured that his self-judgment was entirely unjust and unacceptable to the Board. Still, he remained troubled.

Two days later, on a Wednesday, Collins was scheduled to make an inspection with his trusted assistant, Mr. Brewer. That night, he packed his travel bag and carefully laid out his clothes as he prepared for bed. His wife and family were in Ashtabula at her parents' house where he and his family spent a great deal of time. At home on St. Clair Street in Cleveland, he had come in late, unnoticed by his servant, quartered in the rear of the house. As the train disaster replayed in his distraught mind, his depressed state probably complicated each thought until, at the peak of his insanity, he sat up in bed, placed his revolver in his mouth with the barrel pointing upward, and pulled the trigger, or so it was thought at the time.

Mr. Brewer, his associate expecting to travel with him, never heard from Collins. After two days, Brewer thought he might be in Ashtabula with family. After contacting Collins' family in Ashtabula, learning he was not there, the concerned Brewer went to Collins' Cleveland house. Upon arriving and inquiring, the servant stated that he had not seen Collins in days. In the bedroom, they found Collins' body, the gun still in his hand. He was laid to rest in an impressive, above-ground vault in Chestnut Grove Cemetery in Ashtabula, ironically, not far from the cenotaph memorializing the disaster's "unrecognized dead."

Horrible as it was, the bridge disaster produced many heroes. There were Ashtabula's firemen, the engineer, and the fireman of the Socrates, and the ticket agent, to mention a few. One unlikely heroine was a woman, often overlooked, Miss Marion Shepard of Ripon, Wisconsin. A passenger on the fateful train, she was only slightly injured. Instead of moving to safety to minimize danger to herself, she stayed and assisted others. (See Appendix A.)

A bridge was moved into position to restore rail service to the area, January 17, 1877. Three weeks after the disaster, Friday, January 19, 1877, the burial and memorial service took place for "the unrecognized dead." Had it been warmer weather, the service might have taken place sooner, although body parts were still being turned up. (As late as January 17, 1877, two days before, according to a note in the hand of E. W. Richards, acting coroner, a body was found in the debris.) Arrangements had been made with Associated Press to telegraph an announcement throughout the country three days before the funeral giving sufficient time to reach Ashtabula. A choice burial plot, at the top of a hill above the village, was chosen in Chestnut Grove

Cemetery and paid for by the railroad.

Business was suspended and black crape hung from most doors in Ashtabula the day of the memorial services. Hotels and public buildings were draped in mourning for the victims. A special car was furnished by the railroad for friends and relatives of the wreck's victims, along with railroad officials and Senator Haines. With people arriving by train from different parts of the county, streets became crowded. Most city residents attended.

The services of the day were opened at 12:30 p.m. at the Methodist Church, all congregations of the city taking part. The service opened by singing, "Oh, Think of the Home Over There," by select members of the Congregational, Presbyterian, Baptist, and Methodist church choirs. Prayer was offered by The Reverend I. O. Fisher of the Baptist church. The choir sang "We Are Going Home Tomorrow," a song composed by Philip P. Bliss, killed in the accident. A portion of the forty-ninth Psalm was read by The Reverend John Safford, of the Congregational church. The Reverend White, pastor of St. John's Episcopal Church in Cleveland, made a few remarks, noting the terrible and sudden calamity, and making it a warning for all to be prepared to give up this world, and to be ready to meet their Maker. He was followed by The Reverend Peet, (who was to author the only book on the disaster) formerly pastor of the Congregational church, who spoke of the sacredness of human life. He spoke concerning those whose lives had been graciously spared, having since heard them uttering profane language, and he referred negatively to those who went down to their deaths with gaming cards in their hands. The Reverend James McGiffert of the Presbyterian church mentioned those so badly burned as to be beyond recognition by human eyes, yet recognized by God. After music by the choir, the benediction was pronounced, the service having lasted about an hour. An audience of almost equal size (many attending both services) promptly filled the Episcopal church, where the regular service was conducted.

The funeral procession lined up in front of the churches

in the following order: Marshal Fassett and Coroner Richards; clergy in sleighs; bearers in sleighs; Assistant Marshal; Masonic Association on foot; Mayor and City Council in sleighs; friends and family of deceased in sleighs; St. Joseph Temperance Society; Ashtabula Band; Ashtabula Light Guard; Ashtabula Light Artillery; citizens generally. With relatives of the deceased, out-of-town spectators, and the press from different parts of the country, the procession formed was more than a mile long, probably the largest and most impressive ever seen in the area.

A clearance had been cut through the heavy banks of snow to accommodate the long procession, and once complete, members of the Masonic Order acted as pallbearers. The burial service was opened by the Episcopal church's pastor, The Reverend Moore. A selection of Scriptures was then read by the Reverend McGiffert of the Presbyterian church. Ministers from Ashtabula's other churches presented remarks, and the Masons proceeded with their ritual.

There, at the cemetery atop the hill, in one large lot, nineteen graves had been dug to bury twenty-two bodies and various body parts in nineteen coffins. The coffins were lowered in an emotional moment for the citizens of the little village of Ashtabula, bearing up under a great tragedy, not of their choosing.

The euphemism, "the unrecognized dead," was used to cover several circumstances of victims and their remains. Some bodies and body parts could never be attached to the correct identity or name, even though an individual was known by name to have been on the train. It was likely that some who perished were never known by name, no family or relative ever knew they were on the train, and so no one ever knew to claim their body or personal effects. Others seemed to have vanished, as for example, songwriter Philip Paul Bliss and his wife, Lucy Young Bliss, who were known to have been on the train, but apparently, were cremated in the fire and conflagration, since no trace of a body part or personal effect was ever found. In fact, January 19, the day of the burial of "the unrecognized," three coffins were left at the depot in hopes that relatives coming from out-of-town for the funeral would be able to make an identification. Never named, known but to God, they were buried a few days later in that same plot.

Once the services concluded, it was nearly an hour before everyone got out of the cemetery. Reaching the heart of the city, it was nearly nightfall. Trains were waiting to take out-of-town people back to their hometowns. Citizens of Ashtabula went back to their homes in the solitude of their village, pondering the day's events. For three weeks, Ashtabula had been a center of attention in North America. The people of Ashtabula were ready for normalcy.

The precise number of persons killed in the Ashtabula train disaster will never be known. The total on board the train has been variously estimated. The persons killed that day have been quoted as high as two hundred the day of the disaster, and as low as eighty-seven a few days after the disaster. The official count was ninety-two, but was it the right count?

Bernhart Henn of Buffalo, a passenger conductor for more than five years, testified that he had one hundred sixty tickets in his possession, not including railroad employees traveling on passes. Though he testified that there were only a few children on board, a number of children were found in the wreckage, alive and dead. He also could not be certain of the number of railroad employees on the train. He was not certain how many passengers had got off the train at intermittent stops. After leaving Buffalo, he never took a passenger count. His count of passengers was only his estimate.

Elsewhere in this volume, the technical causes of the bridge failure and the verdict of the coroner and state commission are discussed. Earlier in this essay, the "suicide" of Charles Collins, chief engineer of the railroad company, was described. While in the past, consensus seemed to indicate that Collins committed suicide, medical reports compiled nearly two years later cast doubt on that conclusion. (See Appendices B and C.) However, for reasons unavailable to us, the conclusions of medical analysts who studied the pathology and forensic aspects of Collins' death were never made public. Why the reports were never released, we do not know, but perhaps, the best theory is that they were not made public for fear of further scandal. The train disaster had launched enough gossip. The design of the bridge, the robbery of the dead and survivors, and why the fire was not put out were just a few issues of local comment. There needed to be closure on the disaster, especially for the railroad, which likely did not want the medical analyses released.

Who ordered the reports? Who commissioned and paid for the reports? Why were the examinations conducted almost a year-and-a-half after Collins' death? Who instigated the investigation that required Collins' body to be exhumed for the examination? These are questions without answers now.

One examiner was Dr. Stephen Smith, surgeon to Bellair and St. Vincent's Hospital, New York, and professor of surgical jurisprudence at University Medical College, New York. His signature is at the bottom of the thirteen pages, written in his own hand, and dated June 3, 1878.

He wrote: "On the 26th day of April, 1878, I carefully examined the skull certified to be that of Charles Collins." The doctor's final judgment, in surprisingly blunt terms, was: "Preceding facts properly collected and weighed, justify the conclusion that this man was not a case of suicide." (See Appendix B.)

Another physician, Frank H. Hamilton, M.D., also wrote a nine-page decision on the cause of death, similarly written in his own hand and personally signed. It reached the same unguarded conclusion: "It was not a suicide." (See Appendix C.)

If not a suicide, who murdered Charles Collins? Was it a family member of one of the victims of the train disaster? A surviving victim of the train disaster? Could it have been railroad personnel, seeking to protect themselves? Then, maybe his murder had nothing to do with the train disaster. We will likely never know.

The monument to the unrecognized dead of the Ashtabula bridge disaster was not unveiled until Thursday, May 30, 1895, almost nineteen years after the event. Among the twenty-five names engraved on the monument are hymn writer, Philip Paul Bliss and his wife, Lucy. Many more persons are probably represented in those graves by the various bodies and body parts that ultimately were laid to rest there. (See Appendix D.)

For many years there was nothing to mark the resting place of the unrecognized dead of the train disaster. In 1892, T. W. McCreary, then proprietor of the Hotel James, started a concerted action, which led to the organization of a monument committee and eventually to the erection of a stately cenotaph thirty-five-feet high. Members of the committee were: James L. Smith, president; T. W. McCreary, secretary; Lucien Seymour, treasurer; Norris W. Simons; C. E. Richardson. (Simons was ticket agent on duty the night of the disaster.)

A systematic plan for soliciting funds was instigated, and among the first to respond were President William McKinley, Mrs. James A. Garfield, evangelist Ira D. Sankey, and other notables. Many people came from distant states to be among the five thousand people witnessing the unveiling on Decoration (Memorial) Day, 1895. Speakers at the service were Harry A. Garfield, James H. Hoyt of Cleveland, and Professor P. B. Dodge of Berea College.

The Socrates, front locomotive of the ill-fated train that succeeded in breaking away to safety in the 1876 crash, was on exhibition the day of the unveiling, decked out in colored bunting. It also bore an American flag borrowed from the steamer *Norman,* that had left Ashtabula Harbor the night of the disaster and was lost.

The monument in Chestnut Grove Cemetery was not the only memorial to the train disaster. A bell from the old Lake Street Fire House near 32nd Street was used to call firefighters to the burning wreckage. The two-hundred-pound bell, cast in solid bronze in 1854, is now anchored in front of the fire station on Main Avenue, a gift in 1975 of Mrs. Lena Schlacter of Mt. Clemens, Michigan, a former Ashtabulan.

Over the years, many have claimed to be the last living survivor of the train disaster of 1876. Stories have come from New York to California. One unverified report has some of the last living survivors living as far away as England and Australia. But, who was really the last living survivor of the Ashtabula train disaster?

One of the many claimants, according to an Erie newspaper in 1925, was James F. Hunt, the fireman of the locomotive Socrates, and so identified in the first newspaper accounts immediately after the tragedy. Hunt was nineteen-years-old that fateful night but had already worked for the railroad three years. He was not the last living survivor of the train disaster, but may have been the last railroad worker to have survived.

Probably the most interesting "last survivor" claim was that of Harry Ellsworth Bennett of Philadelphia, Pennsylvania. Mr. Bennett was a candy butcher, as it was called in 1876, on the Lake Shore and Michigan Southern Railway, selling on board, newspapers, magazines, cigars, candy, and sundries. On the night of the disaster, he claimed to have been badly injured. His story was that after helping a lady save her husband, he was so badly injured that he had to be pulled up the side of the gulf on a sled. After being taken to one of the hotels in Ashtabula, the doctors transferred him to a hospital in Cleveland, where he supposedly spent ten months in the hospital. When the railroad adjustment agent came to see him, he saw the condition of Bennett, thought he was not likely to live long, and offered him a dollar a day for the rest of his life. Not much in today's terms, but considering that most men never earned a dollar a day in wages at the time, it was a tidy sum. The agreement was made, and Bennett eventually left the hospital and claimed to have been paid over twenty-four thousand dollars. (See Appendix E.)

Effie Neely died at the age of 101 in Troy Township, Geauga County, Ohio in 1960 and is buried in Jackson, Ohio, where she was born. The last-living survivor identifiable at present, she may not have been the last survivor. Effie Neely was eighteen when the disaster occurred. However, there were children and infants on board that night who did survive. Many of them in 1960 would have been in their eighties and as young as eighty-three. Unfortunately, the passenger list did not list names of children. They were only listed as children of their parents. For this reason, no one can say with certainty who was the last survivor of the train disaster.

Who's Who?
Identifying Victims of the Disaster
Barbara J. Hamilton

Barbara Hamilton is a history and travel columnist for the *Jefferson Gazette* of Jefferson, Ohio. Her curiosity with the Ashtabula train-wreck began when she discovered more than 150 documents, letters, and newspapers, related to the disaster lying dormant in the basement of the Jennie Munger Gregory Memorial Museum that houses early Ashtabula County memorabilia. She continues to be an active participant in telling the Ashtabula railway-bridge story by assisting with an audiovisual program for children and adults.

Without the aid of modern communication systems, rescue services, or assistance agencies, such as The Salvation Army, American Red Cross, the Federal Emergency Management Agency, families and friends of those on board the train that fateful December 29, 1876, were at the mercy of the mail, newspapers, and telegraphy. Many did not hear of the accident until days later. Some did not know if their loved ones were on that particular train. For years afterward, stories abounded of individuals who were supposed to be on that train, but were fortunate that some event kept them from it. Rail schedules were slow and often changed, and a passenger list was not required. In fact, a precise count of persons on the train, even killed in the tragedy, has been impossible. With forensic science in its early stages and the limited skills available in a small town, a number of factors hindered the identification process: lack of a passenger manifest, the decision not to use water to put out the fire that destroyed so much and so many, looters, and the lack of communication among key personnel, as well as limited communication capacities.

As the tragic news was tapped out on the telegraph and shared through the front pages of newspapers, including New York and Chicago dailies, fear struck the hearts of persons waiting for the homeward bound. As days passed, fading hopes turned to dread and then to the stark realization that a family member would never return. Some were able to go to the scene, but extreme weather conditions, finances, distance, and family circumstances prevented most from doing so. Children were missing parents. Wives and husbands were missing their mates. Mothers were missing sons and daughters.

But in faraway Ashtabula, Ohio, some passengers would be forever unidentified. Those bodies that had fallen into the waters of the Ashtabula River that night were best preserved, while those trapped in the cars or nearby were almost completely consumed by fire.

Survivors told of one woman, whose upper body was outside the passenger car, but whose legs were pinned in the wreckage. She cried out to rescuers to cut her limbs off to escape the encroaching flames. Unable to reach her, rescuers watched helplessly as she was consumed by the fire.

In addition to fire, another factor that prevented identification was the preying upon bodies by ruthless persons who arrived at the scene and helped themselves to the effects on or near the bodies. Assuming no one would ever know what was missing or where items could have fallen, the temptation for stealing was present then as it is today at times of disaster.

J. W. Smith of Toronto, Canada, of the firm of Smith Brothers, printers, was known to have had on his person a gold watch and chain, and in a single pocket, a registered letter, a telegram, and seven thousand dollars cash. He also had a revolver on his hip. After the accident, his body was located. The revolver was undisturbed, and the single pocket with the letter and telegram was beside him, but not the seven thousand dollars. The gold watch and chain were also missing. The *Ashtabula Sentinel* (January 11, 1877) called the incident "another indication of the presence upon the disaster of experienced robbers."

The Discovery of Lost Letters

The greatest number of conserved letters are from passengers's families. Reading newspaper accounts, they looked for a name from Ashtabula—an undertaker, the coroner, head of the coroner's inquest, a juror, even eyewitnesses—any name to whom they could address a request for help in identifying or confirming the status of their relative.

These letters, recently uncovered at the Jennie Munger Gregory Memorial Museum at Geneva-on-the-Lake, Ohio, had apparently been unread for decades. They described individuals's hair and eye color, clothing, jewelry, possessions, birthmarks, and scars. They usually described a possible passenger's hometown or point of origin, destination, and their reason for travel.

Excerpts from long-unknown originals, found in the Jennie Munger Gregory Memorial Museum, give warmth and humanity to what may often seem a mere historical event. The letters referenced here are transcribed as they were written, with misspelled words and often with little or no punctuation. (Text or punctuation added or modified is indicated by brackets.)

A New York man, although a very poor speller, gives an explicit description of his brother and his effects. Not knowing anyone in Ashtabula, he pleads that the postmaster deliver his letter to someone who can help.

January the 12 1877
   William W. Forbes started December the 27 about ten o'clock from Chatham village in the evening for Albany said that he was a going to take the first train from Albany to Checarga [Chicago] and from their to St Lewis. he has light brown mustash and chin whiskers. his chin whiskers shorter than his mustash. has blew eyes, has a mark over his right eye and a mark between his lower lip and chin which had been cut. and has black culered clothes and had flat feet. his heels was smashed down in his feet when he was small. the hair on his head was light brown. he said when he started that he was agoing to have his mustash and whiskers cut off and had coarse boots on and well worn was bought last summer had a pair of buckskin gloves and was all pine pitch, ahandling pine timber. and a black common hat had when he started from Chattham village. a little over

one hundred & twenty five dollars in money in a leather pocket book well worne had Maggie A. forbes name in said pocket book. Spencertown, Columbia Co., Ny and isacc Clark name, spencertown, and William hunter, Chatham village, Henry Rivenburgh, Ghent, Col. Co. NY. he had a letter in his pocket from St lewis and lucy ville forbes name scribeled on it. had a light brown over coat, well worn. we think that he was in that terrable axcident happened with the cars that fell through the bridge and number of lives lost if they is any such man hurt or killed please let me now or any such man around thair or ben thair through this terrible axcident.

Mr. postmaster I doon't now your name but if you will rite and let me now wether said man William W. forbes is thair or not I will try and do as mush for you if I ever can.

Yours truly,

Edward W. Rivenburgh, Spencertown, Columbia Co., NY

give me an anser as soon as you can possibly and wether he is berried or not.

Dr. George Hubbard, of Polk City, Iowa, was identified by his brother, on the basis of unusual evidence. For Christmas that year, his mother had woven for him two pairs of socks. After his mother wrote about the hand-knitted socks, crews subsequently found a portion of a leg with the underwear tucked into a hand-knit sock. "By this description a limb, which had been saved from burning with the remainder of the body by lying in the water, was identified as his (Dr. Hubbard's), and taken home for burial" (Stephen D. Peet, *The Ashtabula Disaster,* p. 114).

From Springfield, Ohio, the superintendent of a public school, Henry G. Rogers, and his new wife had gone to Niagara Falls to be married, the Tuesday before. Preparations had been made for their joyful return home, when friends received news of the accident and fearing the worst, immediately sent a dispatch, inquiring whether the superintendent and new wife were on board. Anxiety intensified when word came back that they had, in fact, been on the train. Two men went at once to the site, carrying the concern of each school class. But Sunday, a dispatch was read at church confirming, and then other dispatches followed, announcing that Mr. and Mrs. Rogers had been burned to death, and no portion of their bodies or effects were recovered. A special meeting of the school board was called for appropriate action, and a "depressing sense of great calamity came home to all. A deep gloom was cast over the whole city and mainly put an end to the festivities of the New Year's day."

Correspondence between the Brunner family and the coroner shows the process families utilized to identify their lost loved ones to confirm their deaths, and to find and claim any "relics" (salvaged belongings). Mr. Brunner, apparently a merchant of some standing, assumes (correctly, as it turned out) the loss of four family members, and sends an explicit description of each.

> Having seen a notice in the different papers of certain articles found belonging to the victims of the Ashtabula disaster, I lost four of my family there and nothing of them has been found to identify their bodies by persons sent out from our place except a baggage check No. 1292 Bethlehem, Pa. To Chicago via LakeShore, pretty well melted.
>
> My son Charles, his wife Mattie, his son Henry and daughter all lost and not a vestige found. Mr. Brunner had a gold watch, gold chain with a small opera (double) glass attached, a breastpin being a 2" gold piece bracelet with chain like hanging to it, gold sleeve buttons marked B. Lotti, had a doll Gutte Perchia Head, middling large, dressed in a silk dress.
>
> Henry and Lotti I made a present of a large silver dollar before they left. Charles had a watch with a hair chain. Our watchmaker told me that it was his practice whenever he repaired a watch to take down the number and had a book expressly for that purpose so that he could tell stolen watches, Charley's number was 45912 as he repaired the watch he gave me the number. My son had about $300 on his person about one half in gold in a girdle around his person. They all had their natural teeth.
>
> Chas. was dressed in dark cloth, new overcoat. Lotti in a blue dress material, Mattie, a red dress, black overskirt, a grey felt bonnet with a feather. I think this is all the description I can give you of our children.
>
> I remain yours,
> Samuel Brunner
> Bethlehem, Pa. Feb. 26 1877

Later, the grieving father writes, seeking further confirmation of the loss of his son and family.

Bethlehem, Pa. Feb. 26 1877

Mr. Richards,
At the disaster of the Ashtabula Bridge, my son, his wife and two children perished and not a rag of them found by the friend I sent but now the request I have of you is to know whether the coroner jury has rendered a verdict or not and if so whether you could just get a paper and send it to me. Am willing to pay you for the trouble.

Yours,

Samuel Brunner
Bethlehem, Pa

At the bottom of the letter is penned a response, initialed by E. W. Richards, Ashtabula's kindly acting coroner: "when verdict was rendered sent it on to him. EWR"

Later, a request came by Western Union Telegraph Company from the administrator of the Brunner estate:

Charles E. Brunner and family were killed and burned past recognition in the late Ashtabula accident. Will you have his name mentioned in verdict of coroner's jury as killed or supposed to have been killed. I want this to aid in making proof of loss under life insurance policy upon his life.

P. A. Orton

If neither a body nor any personal effects could be identified, proof that a person was in the accident could not be established, and the name was not listed in the coroner's roster. Therefore, a family could not verifiably claim that a person had actually died.

Almost a year later, Mr. Brunner received the following kind and sympathetic letter from E. W. Richards, acting coroner, which helps explain the confusion and delay in identification.

October 29, 1877
Bethlehem, Pa.

Dear Sir,

Your favor of 26th is just to hand I have the watch, badly burned, #45192 and that is all I have seen of the articles you mention it was fished up out of the creek, and I will send it to you by express if you say so there was a pair of sleeve buttons marked "B"-recently claimed by Mrs. Bradley of Chicago (wife of Wm. Harrison Bradley) she was on the train and was laid up here some weeks and went home without examining the relics at the time you recollect she lost her nurse and child who were in the sleeping cars and not a vestige of them ever found I have not seen any of the other articles you describe-there has never been a doubt in my mind that there was some fearful plundering done during the first confusion and before a regular watch was set over everything. At the same time I must bear my testimony to the strict integrity and conscientious discharge of duty of every R. R. employee that I came in contact with. Mr. Payne, superintendent, was on the spot in a few hours after the accident and was unremitting in his efforts to bring order out of the chaos that prevailed. I have never known a more tempestuous night than that of the 29th of Dec. last.

The strongest men couldn't travel through the snow 5 rods without halting to recover breath. We were without a coroner in the county and I was requested by several of our citizens to take it upon myself and I did not arrive at the scene of the accident until 36 hours after it occurred when I found the best arrangements made by the railroad men that could be under the circumstances.

There were very few citizens at the time aware that the coroner who had been elected had not qualified, which accounts for the delay in organizing a coroner's jury. There was a Mr. Orton, administrator of your son's estate here several months ago, who, with his wife, looked over all the relics. I don't think he claimed anything as I have no record of his doing so. I will write to Mr. Freeman, general baggage agent at Cleveland and enclose your letter, He was on the ground and performed invaluable services for which myself and the public generally ought to be grateful. He may refresh my recollection on some points which I have forgotten or do not know of and in such case will write you again with much respect.

E. W. Richards.

Upon receiving the remains of the watch, Brunner wrote a poignant response.

Your kind letter was duly received and we all thank you for the trouble you had taken. The relic is very valuable to the family. I took it to the watchmaker and the number corresponds to his book of entry and there is no doubt but that it is the identical watch he repaired for them. Once more we thank you very kindly. The enclosed please accept as a present for your trouble.

Samuel Brunner

There is no way to know what was "the enclosed" sent to Mr. Richards "for your trouble."

Another family unable to come to the site, was looking for a handsome, well-dressed brother, a mother's favorite son, traveling first class.

Winchester, Mass. Jan. 3rd 1877
E W. Richards, Esq.

Dear Sir:

I learn by the paper that you have summoned a jury to investigate the horrible accident at Ashtabula. Knowing no one in your vicinity I take the liberty of writing in regards to my brother who we suppose was on that train, presuming that you would in the course of your official duties be better able to give the information than could be derived from any other source. I have been confined to the house by a badly sprained ankle and therefore would be useless as a seeker after my brother's remains. He left my house a week ago today and bade us goodbye, but was uncertain when he should start he made arrangements to go to California.

I learned for the first time today that he started on the through train from Boston at 6 p.m. last Thursday. That he was heard from at Rochester on the same train and there seems to be no reasonable doubt that he was on the train which met with the accident.

I supposed he started earlier and got by the scene of the accident. I took counsel of my hopes. I have not seen his name among the list of killed or wounded. We have heard nothing from him since the accident and therefore conclude that he is among the lost who have either not been found or not recognized.

It seems useless to add to the number of unsatisfied visitors at Ashtabula and so I take what might seem to some a cruel heartless method of ascertaining information about my brother. I have no doubt however that his loss will be mourned as sincerely as some others whose relatives are more demonstrative in their grief.

My brother's name was William F. Wilson of Boston, age 38, next month, 6 ft. high, well proportioned, and fine looking, would naturally attract attention.

His features were very regular and somewhat small for a person so tall, dark moustache and small side whiskers, dark brown hair with a few gray hairs to be seen upon close inspection, good teeth and white.

Generally he wore fine men's underclothing, boson shirts with gold studs and collar buttons, no buttons other than gold on his linen shirts. Sometimes he wore jet sleeve buttons with monogram "W". Leather boots of the unusual length of leg, dark woolen coat vest and pants and all I believe of the same material.

A gold watch made by the Harvard Watch Company of Boston. He had a lot of postal cards with him directed to his friends which he was intending to mail during his journey to inform them where he was. He was unmarried. He wore a navy—overcoat.

He had a first class passage in the Pullman car and we suppose was in the sleeping car at the time of the accident.

He was his mother's oldest son and her favorite and the sad news will bear hardest on her. It would be a great comfort to her to know that his body could be recovered and placed in our family burial lot where she could plant the flowers of spring and when she is called from this earthly sphere her bones could rest near him.

I know that you will be overrun with inquiries, and therefore trespass upon your time and patience with longing lingering hope that you may be able to give us some comforting tiding of our lost one.

I have considered it almost useless at this late day to send any person on to look after my brother. But if you have any encouraging news as to the probable recovery of his body, I would start a person at once upon receipt of a telegram from you.

Of course, telegraph at my expense here. I hope you will find time to write me, even if the tidings are to the effect that should destroy all our hopes.

Very truly yours,

John T. Wilson

Before Mr. Wilson could mail his letter, he received additional news and added it as a postscript to the above letter. The response indicates the degree of confusion that surrounded all reports.

For example, here, as in several other accounts, reference is made to the children and/or family of hymn writer Philip Paul Bliss. However, while Bliss and his wife perished in the accident, they had been unaccompanied by their children.

> News has just come that my brother was on the same car with Prof. Bliss and family. You may be able from that information to gather more successfully some crumbs of consolation for us. J.T.W.

In one instance, grandparents had given their grandson a Christmas present of a musket, just days before the accident. That musket became the item they hoped might identify their grandson and help to confirm the deaths of father (their son) and son (their grandson), who were traveling together. Another son claimed the duplicate receipt.

> From Buffalo, New York to E. W. Richards
> Esteemed friend:
>   Your kind note of the 31st and you have my heartfelt gratitude for the interest you say you will make. As regards evidence of my son and grandson being on the ill fated train is the affidavits of our family who saw them leave and the part of our son's overcoat with letter found and which my son says he thinks you gave a duplicate receipt for.
>   The only thing found of him. My grandson had a regular musket given him on Christmas which he was taking home to Chicago. Our only memento of him.

One letter, in relatively primitive legal language, was from a man looking for the diamond ring of his brother, and he met with success as the receipt indicates.

> Eugene Steindal being duly sworn says that he is the administrator of Robert Steindal, deceased, who died at the Ashtabula disaster, that the said Robert Steindal was descendant brother—and in his lifetime wore a diamond ring. That descendant frequently saw said diamond ring on the finger of Robert Steindal—it was a gold ring set with five diamonds in a line horizontal.

That the ring was found and claimed is evident from the following receipt issued to the family's representatives.

Rec'd Ashtabula Mar. 21st 1877 of E. W. Richard, acting coroner the above described "diamond ring." Hall Brothers for Steindal.

We can never be certain, but the ring might have been the one described in the *Ashtabula Sentinel,* January 11, 1877:

A single arm was found among the debris, on a finger of which was a fine ring, which it was supposed might lead to identification.

Other correspondence:

The Miss Maggie Lewis whose part remains were found and forwarded to St. Louis to her mother left here under the care of my son John D. accompaning this letter I send you a paper unto the account to the memorial service.

The body of Maggie L. Lewis of St. Louis Mo. Identified by Richard Edge of Buffalo, N. Y. by an underskirt, part of a blue waterproof that she wore all of the body left was a part of the leg delivered on the 31st December 1876 Richard Edge

Rec'd Ashtabula March 23/77 from E. W. Richards, acting coroner a burnt and damaged revolver marked "Keoph— and Allen belonging to Dr. Geo. F. Hubbard of Iowa."

Since identifying papers and property became separated from the individuals on the train during the crash, bodies would inadvertently be given names of a survivor, or a wounded person would be given a dead person's name.

Few requests for help resulted in a reply that said the passenger was alive but injured. One particularly poignant letter written two weeks after the accident from a distraught mother read:

Tanners Station, Ind., Owen Co
Feb. 8 1877

To the coroner having charge of the killed and wounded of the Ashtabula Rail road axcident:

Dear Sir:

My son, Charles Patterson left here a short time before the axcident and has not been heard from since We suppose he was perhaps on rout home for Philadelphia. He is a short stout young man, 25 years old, light-complection, light hair, smooth face, had a skar on right temple or just over it. A small speck in rite eye. I find him in the list of partly wounded but no description given and his residence was not given. Any information you can give will be very thankfully received and if thair shold be any one else that had charge please confer and give me any information you can. You will confer a grait favor on me by letting me hear from you.

I am yours very respectfully,
Jesse Patterson

It may be the only surviving letter that ends in relief and joy for the inquisitor. The reply was, "young man wounded and went home. EWR."

One of the undertakers assisting at the time of the disaster was John Ducro, whose Ashtabula funeral business continues in the Ducro family today. Present owner, Peter Ducro and family, have known the legend that their ancestor John had been on the scene and aided in the rescue of victims. But no one in the family had tangible evidence confirming that fact. To the delight of the Ducro family, one simple slip of paper, recently found, reads:

Body identified by her mother and other relatives and claimed by them—John Ducro as undertaker to forward the remains.

On the back of the slip, is the name of one who perished, probably the individual whose remains John Ducro forwarded, Annie Ketlerville (perhaps, Kitterville or Ketterwall), of Beloit, Wisconsin.

False Claims

Some letters were from individuals hoping for financial gain or to collect a memento of the disaster. The shrewd coroner and helpers receiving the letters could usually detect the false request and write "fraudulent" across the letter. A crafty individual would know what to request by reading newspaper reports of "relics" (as they were called) found. One woman wrote:

I have been looking these ten long months to find a little token that I could. He had a gold watch, very nice chains one for the other. Mr. Coroner, if you will send those things that I mentioned and the pictures of the two men, one standing the other—I will return them or bring myself in hast for the answer.

Mrs. B. J. Hudson

At the bottom of the letter is the comment, "suspected as fraudulent E. W. Richards."

Gathering the effects of passengers and returning them to rightful owners or families was an impossible task. Even in such mournful circumstances, unscrupulous individuals sought to take advantage. Reading in the papers of items found, they would write to claim the items for themselves. Only the sharp instincts of the coroner caught these deceitful persons. Some requests were judged suspect and so marked.

Mistaken Identity

One woman wrote to say she had survived the disaster and returned home only to discover her name in the paper as one of the "identified victims." The news clipping read:

> The Ashtabula victims were buried to-day. A body supposed to be that of "Miss Hamlin Lafayette, Indiana," is among the number.

From Lafayette, Indiana, Miss Hamlin wrote January 20, 1877:

> Mr. J. L. Forman:
>
> Dear Sir:
>   Would it make any particular difference in the adjustment of my claim if you would send to us my locket and chain which you now hold? If not, I wish you would please send it me by express. As it must be much charred please pack carefully in cotton that I may receive in as perfect a condition as possible.
>   I clip the enclosed paragraph from our daily paper. Is it possible that one of those poor unfortunates is thought to be me? If so, I wish you would undescribe the committee at once and if

the body is in anyway marked by name please correct, as I could not live thinking another had been buried in my name, No, thank the Almighty Father I was spared that dreadful calamity.

Yours,

Mrs. Ettie Hamlin

One report admitted that the supposed remains of The Reverend Dr. A. H. Washburn, the distinguished rector of Grace Church, Cleveland, "prove not to be those of that gentleman. His clothing, and especially his under-clothing, settles the question in the minds of the friends of the deceased" (*Ashtabula Sentinel,* January 11, 1877).

Yet another example was in the January 3, 1877, *Ashtabula News,* which reported that "Perry Lundin, whose body was identified as above reported, arrived here afterward alive and safe, not having been on the train."

Those Who Survived

Judson Martin and his wife from East Avon, New York, were seriously injured but survived along with their two children. They were seated a third of the way back in the first passenger car. More people survived from that car than any other, probably since it landed upright and was not hit by other cars. Two features of the Martins' experience are especially noteworthy. First, the Martins had just purchased a farm from H. N. Bancroft in the area known as East Union and were on their way to Jefferson to take possession of their new property. According to the *Ashtabula Sentinel* (January 4, 1887), "He first escaped, and then his wife was extricated from the wreck, and as soon as she was on shore she shrieked for her children, who were clinging to a platform in the midst of the stream, and through the heroism of some one, they were rescued." The second involves discovery of the youngest survivor of the crash. In one of the hotels, bars, or homes opened up to victims of the crash, Saturday morning, just hours after the train crash, Mrs. Martin gave birth to a baby boy. In the delicate language of that day the newspaper's front page reported, "Mrs. J. M. Martin, one of the survivors, was prematurely confined today. It is thought the child will live" (*Ashtabula News,* January 3, 1877). In the horror of death, the joy and hope of new life had sprung forth: but sadly, the baby died a few days later. At the end of the month, the *Ashtabula News* (January 31, 1877) noted that "Mr. J. M. Martin and family, who were injured by the railroad accident, were last Saturday able to be removed to Lenox, where they had purchased a farm. Mrs. Martin had to be carried on a bed."

Tradition seems to indicate at least one other birth in the midst of the tragedy. J. E. Burchell, Chicago businessman and survivor of the wreck, who reported extensively on what he witnessed, wrote of "One lady, whose foot had been crushed, was carried shrieking in labor pains to the little hotel, and during the night she gave birth to a child" (D. W. Whittle, ed., *Memoirs of Philip P. Bliss,* p. 295). The *Ashtabula Telegraph* (January 5, 1877) reported along with other events the night of the fire: "A woman, with a dislocated shoulder, and advanced in pregnancy, soon after being taken care of, gave birth to a child—since dead—the mother likely to recover."

Correspondence between the Lawyers and Those Called to Testify

Everyone who could shed some light on the disaster was called to testify before the Coroner's Jury. Suspicion was cast on the railroad, even the molders and fabricators of the iron. The Wrought Iron Bridge Company of Canton, Ohio, produced trusses, arches, and swing bridges. The president and chief engineer, J. Abbott, was called to testify concerning the advisability of using all iron construction on the bridge across the gorge. He wrote the foreman of the jurors of the inquiry, H. L. Morrison:

> I noticed by the report of Hilton's testimony that he does not figure much better for the (Railroad) Co. than I did, in fact,

not quite as well as I did, as I understand he figures iron weight more than I do which would strain the iron that much more from dead weight.

Mr. Hilton, like many others, wrote letters through their lawyers or others offering excuses to hold off their testimony. Many feared the public's wrath and sought to avoid responsibility for a part in the disaster. Hilton's lawyer responded to a request by E. W. Richards, acting coroner:

Mr. Hilton has to make a further examination of the bridge before testifying. As he has to go to New York tonight he may not be able to testify for the present.

James Newell

Amasa Stone was requested to testify, but through his lawyers, he claimed to be prevented by ill health. Public outrage at the accident caused many to refuse or to delay their testimony.

Cleveland, Ohio
Jan. 14th 1877

To Whom it may concern:

This is to certify that Mr. Amasa Stone is under my professional care and that his physical condition is such as to make it impossible for him to leave the city at present.

Very respectfully,
D. B. Smith, M.D.

Charles Paine, general superintendent, received the following note from Amasa Stone's lawyer.

L. S. Sherman, Esq.

Dear Sir
I enclose the letter of Mr. A. Stone in replying to my note informing him of the wish of the jury of inquest that he would attend upon there. His health is so critical that I believe it might

do him serious harm to come there, altho' he says he will do so. Could not his evidence be taken by comission at Cleveland and he be spared the danger of the trip?

Yours truly,
Charles Paine

Whether his health was truly a valid reason for not going to testify, we will never know. But following the disaster and the death of his son, Adelbert, Amasa Stone took his own life seven years later. According to a Western Reserve Studies Symposium, organized by Professor Gladys Haddad, of Case Western Reserve University in 1994, "in 1876, Stone was publicly scorned and held responsible by a coroner's jury for the death of nearly two hundred people in the infamous Ashtabula train disaster. This event might have precipitated Stone's suicide in 1883."

Changes in Identifying and Caring for Disaster Victims Today

What happened after the Ashtabula train disaster would not occur today. Training and preparation for emergencies take place long before disasters occur. Emergency personnel are more professional and more numerous than in the 1870s. Passenger lists and personal identification papers were unheard of then, but a way of life today. Triage is established immediately and emergency vehicles, 9-1-1, sophisticated communication, clinics, hospitals, insurance, far more police and fire personnel, and even the National Guard tend to make accidents more manageable, dreadful though they are.

However, rescuers that night in 1876 had none of these modern advantages. They were merely volunteers or onlookers, unprepared for an emergency of such scope. The disaster has often been referred to as "the perfect disaster" because, if a person did not die from falling, he died from the crash; if not dying from the crash, he died from drowning; if a person did not die from drowning, he died from burning. There was also the dark of night, heavy snow, severe cold, height (the bridge), mechanical power (the train), and water. No one alive at that time had ever experienced the horror witnessed that night, as have few since. They did the best with what they knew, and with the resources available, at that time and under the circumstances.

Families and friends, who wrote the "lost" letters so recently found, were at the mercy of those handling the identification, and true mercy is what they received.

The Loss of Bliss in Ashtabula
Thomas E. Corts

While visiting family one summer day in the early 1990s, Tom Corts happened upon a copy of P. P. Bliss's *Memoirs* in the used bookshop on Ashtabula's Main Avenue. He bought the book having first learned of Bliss from The Reverend John Thomas, a former pastor of Ashtabula's First Baptist Church when Corts was a child. Through the years, Corts's interest intensified in Bliss and the disaster, and led to his compilation of this book.

The most famous of the ninety-eight persons who died in the Ashtabula train disaster of December 29, 1876 was Philip Paul Bliss (1838–1876). He and his wife, Lucy Young Bliss, perished when the bridge gave way, dropping the train more than seventy feet, igniting an inferno so intense that it cremated a number of passengers on the spot,[1] without a trace of their bodies or their belongings ever found.[2] They were among those whom no evidence could identify, remembered by the good citizens of Ashtabula with a monument erected nearly nineteen years afterward "to the unrecognized dead" in the city's Chestnut Grove Cemetery. It was an abrupt end to a remarkable life that softly and tenderly made an enduring mark on the Christian church and the world.

---

1 D. W. Whittle (ed.), *Memoirs of Philip P. Bliss* (New York, 1877), is the most basic document available concerning Bliss. Whittle had access to Bliss's diaries and letters.

2 Numerous accounts of the Ashtabula train-bridge disaster have been rendered. The only full treatment, rushed to press in 1877, was the compassionate account of The Reverend Stephen D. Peet, who personally interviewed many survivors and wrote the book, *The Ashtabula Disaster* (New York, 1877). Peet called it "the greatest railroad disaster on record" (Preface) and devoted an entire chapter to P. P. Bliss, pp. 183–196. As recently as June, 2002, Eric Scigliano in *Technology Review, MIT's Magazine of Innovation,* cited "10 Technology Disasters," pp. 48–52, and included "The Ashtabula Creek Bridge Wreck," p. 51, of December 29, 1876, as "the United States' deadliest bridge collapse."

A Pennsylvania farm boy with little formal music training and minimal schooling, in his very short life, Bliss composed secular and sacred sheet music that sold thousands of copies, and he had a part in the most successful religious songbooks ever published. If, as one scholar asserts, "Gospel hymnody has the distinction of being America's most typical contribution to Christian song,"[3] Bliss is arguably among the most typical contributors. He was the first to use the phrase "Gospel Songs" in a title.[4] Among the earliest gospel songs to gain wide popularity in Britain and America were Bliss compositions. In the span of only twelve years (1864–1876), before his death at age thirty-eight, he was inspired to write "Hold the Fort!," "Almost Persuaded," "Let the Lower Lights Be Burning," "Hallelujah, What a Savior!" and the music to "It Is Well with My Soul," as well as many others in Protestant hymnals, more than 125 years later.[5] It was Bliss who "crystallized" in the mind of evangelist D. L. Moody "the power of singing in Gospel work."[6] Moody said of Bliss:

> I loved and admired him. I believe he was raised up of God to write hymns for the Church of Christ in this age, as Charles Wesley was for the church in his day. . . . In my estimate, he was the most highly honored of God, of any man of his time, as a writer and singer of Gospel Songs, and with all his gifts he was the most humble man I ever knew. I loved him as a brother, and shall cherish his memory.[7]

3 Robert Stevenson, *Protestant Church Music in America: A Short Survey of Men and Movements from 1564 to the Present* (New York, 1966) p. 90.

4 David Smucker, "Philip Paul Bliss and the Musical, Cultural and Religious Sources of the Gospel Music Tradition in the United States, 1850–1876." (Unpublished dissertation Boston University, 1981) p. 28.

5 Lists of Bliss's "most popular" songs have varied over the years, fluctuating with the public taste. Moody thought Bliss would never be forgotten for "Hold the Fort!" By the time of the 125th anniversary of his death, the Ten Most Popular Bliss songs were: "Almost Persuaded," "Hallelujah, What a Savior," "I Gave My Life for Thee," "It Is Well with My Soul," "I Will Sing of My Redeemer," "Jesus Loves Even Me," "Let the Lower Lights Be Burning," "The Light of the World Is Jesus," "Whosoever Will," and "Wonderful Words of Life."

6 John C. Pollock, *Moody: A Biographical Portrait of the Pacesetter in Modern Mass Evangelism* (New York, 1963) p. 77. Whittle, *Memoirs of Bliss,* pp. 42; 168–169.

7 D. L. Moody, "Introduction," in Whittle, *Memoirs of Bliss.*

Bliss's fame and popularity were so extensive that, with Moody's endorsement and leadership, more than $11,600 was collected soon after the Blisses' memorial services. The sum of a thousand dollars went to erect an impressive, twenty-two-foot tall cenotaph to their memories in the Rome (Pennsylvania) cemetery, dedicated June 10, 1877, and $10,600 became the corpus of a trust fund for the subsistence and education of the two surviving Bliss children.[8]

Young as he was, Bliss was a figure of international popularity in an age when fame and recognition came much more slowly. The *Advance,* a contemporary Christian publication, stated "in the case of Mr. Bliss, whose hymns and tunes have made him a favorite in thousands of churches and with millions of Sunday School scholars, his mourners, on both sides of the Atlantic, are innumerable."[9]

Growing up mostly around Rome, in western Pennsylvania, just south of Elmira, New York, the Bliss family was rich in heart, but extremely poor. A hard scrabble, transient childhood, followed Bliss from his birth, July 9, 1838, through moves to Kinsman, Ohio from February, 1844 until 1847, and in 1847 and 1848 to Espeyville, Crawford County, and Tioga County, Pennsylvania. The family's mobility and the tough tenor of the times opened up few educational opportunities. We know that Philip Bliss was beneficiary of a meager, puritanical childhood:

---

8 Moody announced the fund-raising at the memorial service in Chicago, a week after the tragedy, suggesting no contribution more than one dollar so that many could participate. Contributions came from thirty-six states and a number of foreign countries, until contributions were stopped. Over a half-million donors, including children from 3,063 Sunday schools, made gifts from one cent to fifty dollars, according to an 1877 article in *The Sunday School Times,* quoted in Victor C. Detty, *P. P. Bliss July 9, 1838—December 29, 1876: A Centennial Sketch of His Life and Work, 1838–1938, with Selected Gospel Hymns* (Wysox, PA, 1938) p. 23. Also, see Whittle, *Memoirs of Bliss,* p. 344. Moody actually announced to the public that the Bliss children had been well provided for and that contributions should cease (*Ashtabula News,* February 14, 1877). Bliss was reported to have left an estate valued at $15,000 and $30,000 in subscriptions, which had been committed to his two children (*Ashtabula News,* February 7, 1877).

9 Quoted in Whittle, *Memoirs of Bliss*, p. 310. Elsewhere in this essay, mention is made of the extensive publication of Bliss's hymns internationally.

Lucy Bliss once said that the first time she met her husband's father "he reproved me for laughing on Sunday." [10] Yet, the son always remembered his father's singing, praying, and reading the Scriptures, and his mother's daily lessons. [11] But he had almost no experience of formal schooling. Early learning the songs of his father, a cheerful, devout, and earnest man who loved to sing aloud, but was never able to earn a minimal living, young Philip whistled and sang his father's tunes, and occasionally "played" them on crude, self-made musical instruments. [12] He did not hear a piano until he was ten. [13] It almost strains credibility to accept his recollection, confirmed by his sister, that at age eleven, he left home to ease the burden on his family, earning his own living in farms and logging camps, fitting in whatever schooling might be possible along the way. His sister remembered the touching scene that day he left home, the sweetly sensitive boy carrying all his clothes wrapped in a handkerchief, and tossing his sister's two pennies over his shoulder as he made his way down the lane, not daring to look back in a final farewell. [14]

From ages eleven to sixteen, his independent existence was disciplined by work on farms, as a cook in logging camps, as a log-cutter and sawmill laborer, work that yielded as much as nine dollars per month with board, and board was his greatest need. [15] In 1850, during one of his brief periods of organized school attendance at Elk Run, as a Baptist minister conducted a revival among the students, Bliss made profession of his faith in Christ. A short time later, in a creek near his home, he was

10 Quoted in Whittle, *Memoirs of Bliss*, p. 27.

11 Whittle, *Memoirs of Bliss*, pp. 17–19. General background information is taken from Whittle's *Memoirs of Bliss*, unless otherwise noted.

12 Whittle, *Memoirs of Bliss*, pp. 16–17.

13 Ibid., pp. 17–18. The incident probably happened when the Bliss family lived in Kinsman, Ohio, and may have involved a Mrs. Bracken, who owned the only piano in town at that time.

14 Ibid., p. 18.

15 Ibid.

baptized by a minister of the Christian church. In reflection later in life, Bliss said his conversion was undramatic because he could not remember a time when he did not love the Savior, feel remorse for his sins, and pray.[16]

During the winter of 1855, Bliss was able to attend school at East Troy, Pennsylvania, in Bradford County. The very next year, 1856, he was hired to teach school at Hartsville, New York in Allegheny County, where he also worked on a farm near Springfield. From that area, he wrote his family of an accident that happened one day when drawing logs with a pair of oxen, an incident that illustrates the rigors of life for an ambitious young man. He was astride a large log, seeking to hook the chain so as to drag it, when the log inadvertently rolled onto his foot and the oxen dragged him about twelve feet before he could get them to halt. Trapped under the weight of the log, after digging the snow from under his foot, he managed to get loose and get himself to the house, suffering a mangled boot, and a very sore foot.[17]

The school year was short, the term ending the first of March,[18] so other work was needed by a teacher. While Bliss must have been an individual of obvious character and maturity, it is a commentary on popular education of that era that, at the end of those brief experiences, in June, 1857, just before his nineteenth birthday, Bliss could be awarded a Provisional Teacher's Certificate by the Superintendent of Bradford County.[19]

With his teaching perhaps confirming his own need for more education, in the fall of 1857, Bliss enrolled in the Susquehanna Collegiate Institute in Towanda, Pennsylvania.

16 Ibid.

17 Letter to friends, March 6, 1856, quoted in Whittle, *Memoirs of Bliss,* p. 231.

18 Ibid.

19 Bobby Joe Neil, "Philip P. Bliss (1838–1876): Gospel Hymn Composer and Compiler" (Unpublished dissertation, New Orleans Baptist Theological Seminary, 1977) p. 18. A copy of the certificate is in The P. P. Bliss Gospel Songwriters Museum, Rome, PA.

While there only a short time, he apparently received some vocal instruction, was noted for his natural gifts, and was predicted to be bound for a musical career.[20] He took algebra, grammar, physiology, and Latin. To pay his way, he admitted being "a kind of chore-boy, but I am not ashamed of it."[21] "I saw wood, bring water, sweep rooms at so much apiece, and am resolved to earn every penny I possibly can honorably."[22] It was a happy circumstance—he could earn his living, and he had an understanding advisor. "Come along to school one, two or three terms, and if you can't pay me now, pay me after you have earned it," the kindly school owner had said.[23]

Throughout his life, Bliss never glossed over his humble origins, always considered himself privileged, and was ever grateful even for his meager growing up. He once wrote his mother, "For whatever of poor advantages, small houses, plain living, threadbare, patched clothing, back woods society, and unpleasant recollections of my childhood I have to cherish, this precious thought—my parents prayed for me, even before I knew the meaning of prayer, and they consecrated me to the Lord and His service."[24] It was a theme he often repeated, especially in letters home. "I am glad and thankful we were always poor."[25]

His time as a pupil was brief, however, for during the winter term of 1857–58, he was the teacher at the district school at Towner Hill in Rome Township. He had sixty-one boys and girls, from ages five to twenty-one, fifteen of whom were named Towner, including Daniel B. Towner (destined to compose the music to "Trust and Obey," "Grace Greater Than Our Sin," "At

---

20 Detty, *Centennial Sketch,* pp. 8–9.

21 Whittle, *Memoirs of Bliss,* p. 232.

22 Ibid.

23 Ibid.

24 Letter to his mother, Feb. 19, 1871, quoted in Whittle, *Memoirs of Bliss,* pp. 234–235.

25 Letter to his sister, October 31, 1970, quoted in Whittle, *Memoirs of Bliss,* p. 234.

Calvary," and many other hymns).[26] In that locale, he met J. G. Towner, father of hymn writer Daniel B. Towner, an old-time singing schoolmaster, and the elder Towner's singing school afforded Bliss his first systematic instruction in music. That same winter, probably under Towner's influence, he attended his first musical convention in Rome, an event that intensified his passion for music, nurtured his talent, and quickened his musical instincts. At the convention, he was fortunate to meet W. B. Bradbury (compositions include "Just As I Am," "The Solid Rock," "Sweet Hour of Prayer," "He Leadeth Me," "Savior Like a Shepherd Lead Us"), leader of the convention, just beginning his ministry as a full-time composer of sacred music. From Bradbury, Bliss took great inspiration—learned from him, highly regarded his musical ability, and admired him. Bradbury was likely the first person Bliss had met whose full-time vocation was Christian music. At Bradbury's death in 1868, Bliss wrote a song he entitled, "We Love Him," and inscribed it, "The children's tribute to the memory of William B. Bradbury." It concludes:

> We love the things that he has loved,
>   We love his earthly name;
> And when we know his angel form,
>   We'll love him just the same.
> We'll love each other better then,
>   We'll love "Our Father" more;
> We'll roll a sweeter song of praise
>   Along the "Golden Shore."[27]

Fresh from an invigorating year that included academic coursework, teaching, his first formal music lessons, and the stimulating experience of his first music convention, in the fall of 1858, Bliss spent some time in Almond, New York, before coming to teach the winter term at the Rome Academy in Rome (Pennsylvania). In that amazing way in which lives are shaped

---

26 Detty, *Centennial Sketch,* p. 9.

27 Ibid., pp. 19–20.

by small decisions, he boarded in the home of a devout Christian farmer and school board member, O. F. Young. The relationship was cozy, and the Youngs allowed Bliss to bring his sister to live in their home, also, in order to gain the benefit of formal schooling. With three sons, three daughters, the visiting schoolmaster, and his sister, Mr. Young, chorister at the Presbyterian Church, had a standing ensemble. In the warmth of the Young family's hearth, with the young people attending singing schools, choir rehearsals and spelling classes together, romance blossomed, and June 1, 1859, Bliss married the Youngs' eldest daughter, Lucy. After the wedding, they remained in the Young household, with Bliss a farmhand for his father-in-law, paid thirteen dollars per month, standard farmhand wages.[28] Bliss marked the year 1860 as extremely important in his life.

That winter, as an independent teacher of music lessons, his own musical limitations became self-evident, fanning the flame of desire to know more. He was frustrated, then discouraged, and almost depressed at his unfulfilled yearning for music education, but without money even to attend the Normal Academy of Music in Geneseo, New York, one of the more extensive traveling music schools so common in that day, and the great event among music lovers of the area.[29]

He later told the story that one day in summer 1860 when only his grandmother-in-law was in the house, he threw himself on an old settee and, not having the thirty dollars the Music Academy required, "cried for disappointment. I thought everything had come to an end; that my life must be passed as a farmhand and country schoolmaster, and all bright hopes for the future must be given up." Grandma Allen told him she had been saving by dropping coins into an old sock for a number of years. Moved by his passion, she counted the coins, found more

---

28 Detty, *Centennial Sketch*, p. 10; Whittle, *Memoirs of Bliss*, pp. 21–22. In Bliss's diary, Whittle found this entry: "June 1, 1859—Married to Miss Lucy J. Young, the very best thing I could have done" (Whittle, *Memoirs of Bliss*, p. 22).

29 Whittle, *Memoirs of Bliss*, pp. 21–22.

than the thirty dollars required, and did a great service for the modern church in underwriting Bliss's six-week course. It was a life-changing time for the young musician, allowing him to meet music leaders of the area, to answer questions he had often posed to himself, and to have the realms of Christian music unveiled. After the course, his father-in-law bought him a twenty dollar melodeon and, he noted in his diary, that with the melodeon and Old Fanny, his horse, he was in business as a professional music teacher.[30]

Income from his music teaching and piano-tuning bettered his standard of living and allowed him freedom to attend the traveling schools again in 1861 and in 1863. Bliss was chosen the most intelligent pupil by his teacher at the first school he attended and thereafter was given the attention reserved for prize pupils, including private voice lessons.

In Bliss's life story, it is difficult to overplay the part the traveling music schools and conventions played in his personal development—first as vital to his education, and then as vital to his livelihood. His lack of formal schooling and music training is well documented. While singing schools date to the early eighteenth century, their rise to prominence in rural areas and in the South in the nineteenth century was remarkable. They became social events, opportunities to straighten out confused music theory, sessions for learning to read music, and short courses in vocal technique. Classes were often held at night, and teachers worked ten-day or five-day schools around the schedules of farm workers. Conventions became social and commercial opportunities, bringing together amateur musical enthusiasts for pleasure and idea-sharing, allowing established authors-composers to meet local aspiring talent, and publishers often sent agents to such events advertising their latest offerings.[31]

---

30 Whittle, *Memoirs of Bliss*, pp. 23–24.

31 For a discussion of singing schools and conventions, see James R. Goff, Jr., "Shape Notes & A Musical Tradition,"(Chapter II), *Close Harmony: A History of Southern Gospel* (Chapel Hill, 2002).

Particularly in the South, such traditions remained popular until pre-World War II years, and one can still meet many people who benefited from traveling singing schools.

The songwriting career of Philip Bliss was launched in 1864. While living in Rome, doing farmwork and teaching music, he wrote "Lora Vale," a mournful, sentimental tune about the dying of a young girl, with the chorus:

> Lora, Lora, still we love thee,
> Tho' we see thy form no more,
> And we know thou'll come to meet us
> When we reach the mystic shore.[32]

It happened that James McGranahan ("There Shall Be Showers of Blessing," "I Know Whom I Have Believed," "I Will Sing of My Redeemer"), himself a hopeful songwriter and musical friend of Bliss, was a clerk that summer in the country store and post office of Rome. McGranahan reviewed the proofs of Bliss's first composition and offered suggestions. Published by Root & Cady in 1864 as sheet music, "Lora Vale" was popular and sold several thousand copies.

In 1863 or 1864, Bliss had met George F. Root (credited with "Jesus Loves the Little Children," "The Lord Is in His Holy Temple") who, with his brother, E. T. Root, had the firm of Root & Cady of Chicago. The Root brothers had early taken note of Bliss, and George Root recalled after Bliss's death,

> [O]ur interest constantly increased in this many-sided 'country boy,' as he called himself. His curious conceits, so piquant and varied, his beautiful penmanship, his bright nature, that could not seem to see anything unhappy or unbeautiful in life, attracted us strongly, and led often to letters on my part that were not needed for business purposes, but were for the sake of the answer they were sure to bring. [33]

Publishing was only one of several Root Brothers musical endeavors that included a retail music store, and traveling music

---

32 Whittle, *Memoirs of Bliss*, pp. 30–31.

33 Ibid., p. 32.

schools throughout the Midwest. While Bliss had been drafted into the army in 1865, he had been discharged within two weeks, as it became clear that the War was ending. With other members of a gospel quartet, called the "Yankee Boys," Bliss accepted the offer of Root & Cady to "come West" to Chicago to hold promotional concerts on a salaried basis.[34] In the context of difficult economic times following the Civil War, we know little about why the "Yankee Boys" idea seemed to wither within about a month of their arrival in Chicago, but the Root brothers retained Bliss.[35] For the next four years with Root & Cady and then later on his own, Bliss earned his living by holding music conventions, giving concerts and music lessons throughout the northern Midwest. Simultaneously, he helped write and assemble songs for Root & Cady publications. Root recognized Bliss's talents, having declared, "Yes, I consider Mr. Bliss as incomparably the rising musical man of our day."[36]

Another pivotal year in Bliss's life came at age thirty, in 1869, when he met D. L. Moody. The evangelist was not quite a year older than Bliss and was yet to reach the pinnacle of international fame that awaited him. He had created a stir locally in Chicago and regionally through his Sunday School work, and had been holding summer meetings in Wood's Museum Theatre, Clark and Randolph Streets in Chicago.[37] In the local setting, Moody's modus operandi was to preach in the open air from the steps of the nearby courthouse for about thirty minutes and then, having attracted a crowd, to urge them into his meeting. Bliss and his wife, having heard of Moody but never

---

34 James Vaughn claimed to have invented the gospel quartet in 1895. He is said to have put the first full-time, professional gospel quartet on the road in 1910. (Goff, *Close Harmony,* pp. 68–69.) It was by quartets that southern gospel publishers promoted their music to people. With the "Yankee Boys," Root & Cady, Bliss, et al., may have been ahead of their time.

35 Whittle, *Memoirs of Bliss,* p. 38.

36 Ibid., p. 320.

37 Ibid., pp. 41–42.

having heard him, out for a summer stroll before Sunday evening services, happened onto the outdoor preaching. When Moody appealed to all to come inside, they followed. Absent a music director that evening, the singing was weak, and from his place in the congregation, Bliss's strong voice and equally strong countenance, attracted Moody's attention. When the service was over and Moody stood greeting folks at the door, Bliss recalled later, "as I came to him he had my name and history in about two minutes, and a promise that when I was in Chicago Sunday evenings, I would come and help in the singing at the theater meetings." Moody asked Root & Cady, "where in the world they had kept such a man for four years that he hadn't become known in Chicago?"[38]

In May of 1870, Bliss accompanied Moody's friend, Major D. W. Whittle, to a Sunday School Convention at Rockford, Illinois. There, Whittle, a major conference speaker, related an incident from the Civil War that had ended only five years earlier to illustrate Christ's being the Christian's commander, His coming to the Christian's relief, and the Christian life as a battle against evil. Just before General W. T. Sherman began his march to the sea, about twenty miles north of Marietta and Atlanta, Confederate troops cut Sherman's communications lines along the railroad at Altoona ("Allatoona") Pass, site of a huge fortification of Union supplies and rations. It was extremely important that the earthen fortification commanding the Pass and protecting the supplies be held. Confederate forces surrounded the works, and vigorous fighting ensued. Outnumbered, the battle seemed lost and the cause hopeless to Union soldiers. But at a crisis moment, an officer caught sight of a white signal flag, twenty miles away, atop Kennesaw Mountain. From mountain to mountain the signal was waved, according to Whittle's retelling, finally being copied as: "Hold the Fort; I am coming. W. T. Sherman." The song was instantly born in the

---

38 Whittle, *Memoirs of Bliss*, p. 42; cf. Pollock, p. 77.

mind of Bliss, and he applied it to paper when he got back to Whittle's home in Chicago.

	Chorus:
Ho! My comrades, see the signal	Hold the fort, for I am coming,
Waving in the sky!	Jesus signals still.
Reinforcements now appearing	Wave the answer back to heaven,
Victory is nigh!	By thy grace, we will. [39]

Though, actually, the expression "Hold the Fort!" was never used—three messages were sent: one saying "hold out," another saying "hold fast," and another saying "hold on"—Whittle's story was in essence correct.[40]

"Hold the Fort!" was published first as sheet music, bringing immense popularity to its author-composer, and making the expression, "hold the fort" a widely used colloquial expression, still in use. In early 1877, Sankey judged "Hold the Fort!" "the most popular sacred song in England or America." [41] A biographical dictionary published a decade after Bliss's death stated that his songs had "made him famous," with "Hold the Fort!" being "his most famous song," its words "sung wherever

---

39 Whittle, *Memoirs of Bliss,* pp. 66–70, p. 43; Popular in the northern U. S. and in the British Isles, "Hold the Fort!" never caught on in the South for obvious reasons. A small volume with elegant artwork engravings, entitled, *Hold the Fort! by P. P. Bliss* (Boston 1877), was "respectfully inscribed" to William Tecumseh Sherman, published in 1877 and sold very well, copies still seen in secondhand bookshops even today. During their southern journey in 1876, Whittle and Bliss journeyed to the top of Kennesaw Mountain from which Altoona Mountain was visible twenty miles away, and recalled the incident and prayed on the site (Whittle, *Memoirs of Bliss,* pp. 66–70).

40 Scheips noted that General W. T. Sherman was unaware of the song until 1875, five years after its introduction, and General Sherman wrote "I do not think I used the word – 'Hold the Fort!'. " Paul J. Scheips, *Hold the Fort! The Story of a Song from the Sawdust Trail to the Picket Line* (Washington, 1971) pp. 22–23. Though Whittle did not witness the events firsthand, he was on active duty in the vicinity of Atlanta at that very time, and under the command of Major General Oliver Howard in October, 1864. More than three decades later, in 1899, General Howard remembered that Whittle had stood beside Sherman as Howard's representative atop Kennesaw during the signaling incident. Whittle, however, never claimed that association, though it seems likely that he would have done so, if it were true. Cf. Scheips, pp. 8–9; Whittle, *Memoirs of Bliss,* pp. 68–70.

41 Whittle, *Memoirs of Bliss,* p. 169.

English is spoken," but with his other compositions "hardly second to that."[42] In the opinion of *Harper's Weekly* magazine, "Probably no modern hymn has been more widely sung in England and America than the one just named ['Hold the Fort!']."[43] Not limited to English, "Hold the Fort!" was translated into nearly all the European languages, into Chinese and the native languages of India,[44] and it was also heard in Swedish and in Zulu.[45] The militant tune and crisp, imperative title could not be contained solely within the religious sphere and, in time, the song lent itself to all sorts of parodies, serving the cause of presidential candidates in the 1876 election, and becoming widely used in prohibition, suffrage, and labor movements. It was included in a labor songbook as recently as the 1950s.[46] One of the parodies of the late 1800s was supposedly created by street people:

> Hold the forks, the knives are coming,
> The plates are on the way
> Shout the chorus to your neighbor,
> Sling the hash this way.[47]

---

42 "Philip Paul Bliss," *Appleton's Cyclopaedia of American Biography,* New York, 1887, Vol. I, pp. 293–294.

43 Quoted in Whittle, *Memoirs of Bliss,* p. 310.

44 Peet quoted Moody as saying he had received a hymnbook with Bliss's hymns translated into Chinese. Peet, *The Ashtabula Disaster,* p. 188. Peet also told of a South African friend who wrote that he was traveling and stopped for a night's rest in Zulu country. He was surprised to hear a company of natives singing "Hold the Fort!" Peet, *The Ashtabula Disaster,* p. 189; *Inter-Ocean* newspaper of Chicago, quoted in Whittle, *Memoirs of Bliss,* p. 298. An editorial in the same newspaper stated, "It is not too much to say that it ['Hold the Fort!'] is popular beyond any other Sabbath School song of the age." Ibid.

45 Mrs. W. F. Crafts (Sara J. Timanus), "Biographical Sketch of P. P. Bliss," in *Song Victories of the 'Bliss and Sankey Hymns'* (Dover, New Hampshire, 1877) p. 153. The Crafts family exchanged letters with the Blisses; cf. Whittle, *Memoirs of Bliss,* pp. 239, 243.

46 Scheips, *Hold the Fort!,* pp. 30–31. Scheips notes that the tune and some of the words formed the basis of a song from the 1950s, celebrating the independence of the African nation of Ghana (p. 34).

47 Scheips, p. 26.

Who knows what influences shaped the warm, simple sincerity that seemed to characterize Bliss's gifts? His impoverished childhood? His father's simple singing? His heartfelt spirituality? In the era of Stephen Collins Foster and extreme sentimentality, he seemed to reach an appealing balance. "Bliss developed a simple poetic style with enough substance and charm to avoid either stiltedness or prattle."[48] Henry Ward Beecher praised Bliss's hymns for not falling into "sentimentalism gone drunk with miserable garbage and trash. . . . He has been a tongue of the Lord."[49]

Following their initial meeting in 1869, the always persistent Moody never ceased urging Bliss to take up full-time evangelistic work, no doubt hoping to link Bliss with D. W. Whittle, on whom Moody was also both preying and praying. Bliss had assumed direction of the choir of First Congregational Church of Chicago in 1870, later becoming superintendent of the Sunday School, roles he filled for the next four years. Such work gave Bliss a tether to a local congregation, while leaving him free to conduct music lessons, schools, and conventions: yet, anchored in Chicago, Moody's home base, he was afforded no relief from Moody's relentless pleadings. From Scotland in 1873–74, Moody sent letters: "You have not faith. If you haven't faith of your own on this matter, start out on my faith. Launch out into the deep." The ever wise counsel of Lucy Bliss was: "I am willing that Mr. Bliss should do anything that we can be sure is the Lord's will, and I can trust the Lord to provide for us, but I don't want him to take such a step simply on Mr. Moody's will."[50] Bliss seemed reluctant, whether, as Whittle opined, because Bliss doubted his ability to be useful as a traveling musical evangelist, or whether he thought the attraction to such work was the result of his own

---

48 Smucker, p. 59.

49 Henry Nash Smith ed., *Popular Culture and Industrialism, 1865–1890* (New York, 1967) p. 511.

50 Whittle, *Memoirs of Bliss,* p. 49.

wishes, rather than an authentic sense of "call."[51]

Having sprung from such extreme poverty, and meeting financial success for the first time in his life, it may be that practical financial considerations held him back. With his business background, Whittle was aware that Bliss's income from his music business was "good and growing." To yield to Moody's suasion, as Whittle noted, was "giving up his convention work," "giving up of income," simply "trusting God for all means of support," "relinquishing of all plans of ever settling down in a home," "lowering of his reputation in the eyes of many well-meaning musical friends," and accepting a calling to hard work and self-denial.[52]

All the while, Moody was applying similar urgings to Whittle, a high-ranking corporate businessman. Almost as an experiment or trial, in March, 1874, Bliss accompanied Whittle to Waukegan, Illinois, for a series of three special meetings in the Congregational church. With both Bliss and Whittle active targets of Moody's powerful prayers and persuasion, it is likely that the great evangelist had a behind-the-scenes hand in the invitation to Waukegan. Though perhaps the dates are confused,[53] Whittle later recalled that when his nearest neighbor and dear friend, attorney Horatio G. Spafford, visited Moody in Britain in 1874 after the tragic loss of four Spafford children at sea, Moody pressed Spafford to return home and persuade both Whittle and Bliss to devote themselves to full-time ministry.[54]

---

51 Whittle, *Memoirs of Bliss,* p. 49.

52 Ibid., p. 51.

53 Whittle, *Memoirs of Bliss,* p. 49, has the date of the Spafford children's deaths and the father's subsequent trip to be with Moody in England as November, 1874, seven or eight months after the date when Whittle and Bliss had gone to Waukegan (March 1874), according to a letter cited by Whittle, *Memoirs of Bliss,* p. 50.

54 Whittle, *Memoirs of Bliss,* pp. 49–50. It was in 1876, when Sankey was visiting the Spaffords in their Chicago home, that Spafford wrote the poem, "It Is Well with My Soul," in commemoration of the accidental deaths at sea of his four children two years earlier. Bliss set the poem to music and sang it for the first time at a meeting in Moody's Farwell Hall (Ira D. Sankey, *Sankey's Story of the Gospel Hymns,* [Philadelphia, 1906] p. 119). Later, Spafford, was designated, with Whittle and The

Whittle had been a Wells Fargo cashier who enlisted in the Union Army, was wounded at Vicksburg in 1863 and, while recovering in Chicago from his wound, he met and fastened a friendship with Moody. Moody had sought to induce Whittle also to end his high-income career as a business executive and to give himself full-time to preaching and evangelism. In the Waukegan venture, both Bliss and Whittle wanted to see if their efforts would be fruitful and if they could detect a sense of calling to full-time evangelistic work. Bliss may have been particularly vulnerable, inasmuch as he had just resigned his position at First Congregational Church. It is unclear what prompted his leaving but, perhaps, in a foretaste of such controversies over music as plague the church in our day, he wrote: "I know not what they'll do. More showy music was demanded, and I resigned. I must insist on plain music for devotion in public worship. And I can have no sympathy with operatic or fancy music for Sunday."[55] In the context of their Waukegan experiment, Thursday afternoon, March 26, an informal prayer gathering of leaders in the study was transformed into Bliss's consecration service. He, "in a simple, childlike, trusting prayer, placed himself, with any talent, any power God had given him, at the disposal of the Lord, for any use He could make of him in the spreading of His Gospel."[56] When the series of services ended, Whittle and Bliss returned to Chicago, Bliss to find someone to take over his music conventions, and Whittle to resign his position as Treasurer of the Elgin Watch Company. As Bliss described the decision to his old music teacher:

[T]he way has been very clearly made known to me and my wife, for my immediate future. We have long prayed God to

Reverend E. P. Goodwin, to serve as trustees of the copyright profits of Bliss's writings (Whittle, *Memoirs of Bliss*, p. 5). Spafford and his wife eventually became much interested in the Second Coming of Christ, eventually moving to Jerusalem with their one remaining daughter to await Christ's return. Mr. Spafford died, shortly thereafter in Jerusalem (Sankey, *Sankey's Story*, p. 119).

55 Letter quoted in Whittle, *Memoirs of Bliss*, p. 241f.

56 Whittle, *Memoirs of Bliss*, p. 51.

lead me into the widest field of efficient labor. . . .[N]ow I am fully persuaded He calls me to give my time and energies to writing and singing the Good News. I am constrained by what Christ is and has been to me, to offer all my powers directly to His sweet service. . . . I am willing—we are willing—to leave ourselves where we always have been, in our Father's loving hands. . . . Major Whittle goes with me to preach the Gospel while I try to sing it.[57]

The Whittle–Bliss combination, in close friendship and association with Moody, worked together until Bliss's death. The young musician and entrepreneur left behind a career with its promise of generous income and rising reputation, that would earn as much as a hundred dollars for a four-day convention engagement. His *Gospel Songs* book came out in 1873–74, while Moody and Sankey were in England. When they returned to the U.S., Bliss's songbook was an inspiration to Sankey and the two worked together.[58] And his *Gospel Hymns and Sacred Songs,* issued in 1875 in collaboration with Ira D. Sankey, almost immediately produced royalties of sixty thousand dollars, a very significant sum. Yet, not a cent came to them, personally. Whittle, who himself later wrote the words to such great Gospel songs as "Showers of Blessing," "Moment By Moment," and "I Know Whom I Have Believed," said Bliss never looked back.[59] After his songbooks were producing great income, mindful that Bliss had sacrificially given up the royalties to allow them to be used for religious and charitable purposes, Moody urged Bliss to

---

57 Letter of March 31, 1874, quoted in Whittle, *Memoirs of Bliss,* p. 257.

58 William Moody, *The Life of Dwight L. Moody* (New York, 1900) pp. 172–173. Businessman William E. Dodge of New York, who chaired the Trust, which used all proceeds and royalties for charitable purposes, noted that by September 1885, songbooks had amassed $357,388.64 in royalties, a very significant sum (W. Moody, p. 174).

59 Whittle, *Memoirs of Bliss.* Financial support of the two men and their families may have been shaky at first. Apparently, Moody urged his church to support them. With his remarkable fund-raising skills, Moody found funds to send to each, including two thousand dollars to Bliss at one time, according to Lyle W. Dorsett, *The Life of D. L. Moody: A Passion for Souls* (Chicago, 1997) p. 199.

take five thousand dollars for himself and his family.[60] Bliss declined. Once during the last summer of his life, someone congratulated Mrs. Bliss on the remarkable sale of *Gospel Hymns and Sacred Songs*, and suggested that it must have provided at least ten thousand dollars toward a home. She is reported to have replied, "Mr. Bliss has not ten dollars to pay down on a home. Since January we have been living from day to day doing the Lord's work with our might and depending upon what he sends us. Although the illness of our children has greatly increased our expenses beyond other years God has sent us enough to supply our needs."[61]

Especially for one who had grown up with so little in life, Bliss was remarkably generous, very responsible about money, but never a passionate accumulator. In 1863, with some of the first money from his successful singing schools, he had managed to save a few hundred dollars and with it bought for his parents a little cottage in the town of Rome, the first home his parents had ever owned. His father told him, "Phil, I never expected to have so good a home on earth as this."[62]

His letters indicate a constant concern for his extended family, for his mother and sisters, and others, but not much concern for money. He promised to pay the tuition of his nephew, later to send him ten dollars per month on the first of each month, and urged the young man to borrow from him, if needed, rather than from anyone else.[63] He pleaded with his sister to tell him what she needed, and he would send it.[64] He reported on turning down a salary of three thousand dollars in

---

60 Crafts, "Sketch of Bliss," p. 153.

61 Ibid., p. 152.

62 Whittle, *Memoirs of Bliss,* pp. 26–27. That same cottage is today The P. P. Bliss Gospel Songwriters Museum in Rome, Pennsylvania.

63 Letters to nephew, Dr. William Jennings, December 11, 1871, November 29, 1872. Quoted in Whittle, *Memoirs of Bliss,* p. 259.

64 Letter to sister, March 9, 1874, quoted in *Memoirs of Bliss,* p. 242.

gold to lead the music in a San Francisco Tabernacle, with the Handel & Haydn Society & Co.[65] The Reverend Dr. Goodwin, pastor of the First Congregational Church, Chicago, who was Bliss's pastor, and with whom he worked, told of Bliss's own personal charity fund, which seemed to be unlimited. Goodwin knew that it yielded as much as one thousand dollars in six months. He also knew what it was to have Bliss put ten dollars or twenty-five dollars into his hand for some use among the poor, and knew that on occasion Bliss had turned over his pocketbook to meet the need of someone in particular distress.[66]

In all, Bliss was responsible for editing seven books of gospel songs, while several collections by others highlight inclusion of his songs. Bliss helped the Root brothers with a few songs in books intended for Sunday Schools, *The Triumph* in 1868 and *The Prize* in 1871. Bliss's first compilation was *The Charm: A Collection of Sunday School Music,* also published in 1871, followed by his *Sunshine for Sunday Schools: A New Collection of Original and Selected Music* (1873). That same year, he published a collection intended for singing schools and conventions, *The Joy: A Collection of New and Carefully Selected Music Classes, Choirs, and Conventions.* In 1872, Bliss's collection of popular and secular songs was issued as *The Songtree: A Collection of New Songs, Duets, Trios and Quartets.*

Bliss's remarkable versatility was appreciated then, as now. One scholar has written that Bliss "was the only nationally known person to combine the major roles of soloist, teacher, composer, compiler and poet." [67]

The songbook, *Gospel Songs,* of 1874 was perhaps the earliest uniting of the descriptor, "Gospel" with "song," as designating a type of song.[68] The title, just as the collection itself, was put

---

65 Letter, December 22, 1873, quoted in Whittle, *Memoirs of Bliss,* p. 256.

66 Quoted in Whittle, *Memoirs of Bliss,* p. 332.

67 Smucker, p. 53.

68 Ibid., p. 28.

together by Bliss on his own.[69] When Moody's music associate, Ira D. Sankey, returned from England where he had introduced a number of Bliss songs (including "Jesus Loves Even Me," which had become so joyously popular as a congregational song in the Moody campaigns),[70] he discovered Bliss's compilation, *Gospel Songs,* and invited Bliss to join him in publishing a new collection. In England in 1873, in response to popular demand, Sankey had published a small pamphlet, *Sacred Songs and Solos,* which included some Bliss songs, and Sankey wrote that the little pamphlet, along with a companion book with words only, had received a wider circulation than any collection of hymns ever published.[71] Their joint effort appeared in 1875 as *Gospel Hymns and Sacred Songs,* followed by *Gospel Hymns No. 2,* in 1876.

Bliss made distinctive contributions to the world of Christian music. He wrote words and music that are still highly valued today and are still included in contemporary hymnals more than 125 years after his death. The scholar, B. J. Neil, has identified 303 sacred pieces bearing Bliss's name as either author, composer, or both. Including secular songs known to have been published, one can attribute at least 398 pieces to Bliss (as author, composer, or both).[72] With his great love of children, he was among early evangelical songwriters to aim gospel music and choruses at children. He helped to popularize gospel music as a separate form, drawing on musical concepts common to "secular" music of the day, employing text not addressed to God, as were traditional hymns, and bearing testimony of personal

---

69 Historian James R. Goff, Jr., claims "The term 'gospel music' first appeared in the late nineteenth century." Neil dates the phrase "gospel music" to 1644 and "gospel hymn" to the early 1800s. Cf. Goff, *Close Harmony,* p. 6 and Neil's dissertation, previously cited, p. 1. Bliss appears the first to use the term, "Gospel Songs," and as a title. With the revival movements of the late 1800s, the linkage of gospel with various musical terms took root in common parlance. Neil, pp. 1–2.

70 Whittle, *Memoirs of Bliss,* p. 169.

71 Ibid. William Moody, *Life of Dwight L. Moody,* p. 172, felt Bliss inspired the idea of publishing gospel songbooks for the masses.

72 Neil, "Bliss," pp 83–84, 165.

experience or the desire for personal experience, expressing a yearning or urging, or placing a "claim" on some future possibility or Scriptural promise.[73]

P. P. Bliss was an attractive, winsome personality— unpretentious, he liked to call himself "country boy." Whittle described him: "Of large frame and finely proportioned, a frank, open face, with fine, large, expressive eyes, and always buoyant and cheerful, full of the kindliest feeling, wit, and good humor, with a devout Christian character, and of unsullied moral reputation."[74] The young musician, F. W. Root said of him, "If ever a man seemed fashioned by the Divine hand for special and exalted work, that man was P. P. Bliss. He had a splendid physique, a handsome face, and a dignified striking presence."[75] "It is rare indeed to find both mind and body alike so strong, healthy and beautiful in one individual as they were in him."[76] Root once said that "Mr. Bliss's voice was always a marvel to me. . . . He would have made name and fortune on the dramatic stage had he chosen that profession and studied a more scientific class of music."[77] And beyond the remarkable voice, Root also recognized his quick, analytical mind. He observed that "His faculty for seizing upon the salient features of whatever came under his notice amounted to an unerring instinct. The one kernel of wheat in a bushel of chaff was the first thing he saw."[78] The Reverend G. C. Waterman, who knew Bliss well before he went to Chicago and secured a high level of fame, said of Bliss: "His personal appearance and bearing were such as to attract

---

73 A discussion of the various concepts of hymn, gospel song, etc., can be found in Smucker, "Philip Paul Bliss and the Musical, Cultural, and Religious Sources of the Gospel Music Tradition in the United States, 1850–1876" (Unpublished dissertation, Boston University, 1981) pp. 9–24.

74 Whittle, *Memoirs of Bliss*, p. 21.

75 Ibid., p. 36.

76 Ibid., p. 32.

77 Ibid., p. 37.

78 Ibid., p. 33.

and win respect and friendship wherever he went. Nature had lavished upon him a profusion of charms. Not Saul or David was more eminent among his fellows for fine physique and manly beauty."[79] Evangelist George C. Needham described Bliss as follows: "In personal appearance, he was a fine specimen of a vigorous man. Large, well-proportioned, noble in presence—he never failed to produce an impression on the passer-by."[80]

He inherited from his father a happy, joyous disposition, which George Root described thus: "His smile went into his religion and his religion into his smile. His Lord was always welcome and apparently always there in his open and loving heart."[81]

The head of the Chautauqua Assembly, J. H. Vincent, who was in constant contact with the important orators, political figures, and divines of that day, described Bliss warmly:

> He had the delicacy of a woman and the strength of a man. His physique was magnificent. I think he was one of the most handsome men I ever met. Large, well-proportioned, graceful, with a fine, manly face, full of expression. . . . One of the holiest, Mr. Bliss was one of the cheeriest of men. His was not a somber piety. There was no touch of asceticism in his nature. He was as simple as a child, and full of genial humor. His personal letters overflow with playfulness, puns, rhymes, and personal thrusts of the wittiest but always of the most generous character. . . . He never had anything but good to say of his brethren. He never carped nor criticized. He saw in others what he had most of in himself. He 'took to' people. He loved his fellow men.[82]

"I never knew a man more thoroughly imbued with the Christian spirit," Vincent opined.[83] It was a sentiment corroborated by a pastor the Blisses knew and visited, when he wrote: "I have long been accustomed to think of Mr. Bliss and speak of him as my ideal Christian gentleman—the most perfect

---

79 Quoted in Whittle, *Memoirs of Bliss,* p. 301.

80 Ibid., p. 307.

81 Ibid., p. 33.

82 Ibid., pp. 72–73.

83 Ibid., p. 72.

specimen I had ever met." [84]

Whittle knew him as "a very systematic and orderly man," "scrupulously neat in person and apparel, and with the sensitiveness of a woman in matters of taste." "A misspelled word in a letter, or the wrong pronunciation of a word in an address, was to him like a note out of harmony in music." [85]

But into all his attributes, he infused a sense of humor. He wrote his mother from the inner city of Chicago to tell her how they arose at six and how they "milk our cow, by setting a pail on the back steps with a ticket in it (8 c[ents] a quart)." [86] Ever fascinated with words, he included acrostics in his songbooks, and often in his teaching, playful word combinations or schema would be on the blackboard to start the class. Among his nonreligious songs are humorous parlor numbers, such as "A Retrospectigraph" and "The Photograph." He referred to his home as "Kot ov Kontentment." [87] His purchase of a piano was described to folks at home as "P Annie." [88] To his nephew, Will, Milwaukee became "Milky Walky" [89] and Montgomery, Alabama became "Mont-gum-or-rye or Gum Mountain." [90] Anticipating singing at a women's temperance mass meeting, he wrote a friend: "I believe in women, prayer, and God, so there's only one side for me in the great crusade." [91] Tending toward the corny by today's standards, it was good humor in that day, and then as now, it was an evidence of a man of joyful outlook who did not

---

84 The Reverend D. W. Morgan, quoted in *Memoirs of Bliss*, p. 321.

85 The Reverend D. W. Morgan, quoted in *Memoirs of Bliss*, p. 59.

86 Letter to mother, February 19, 1871, quoted in Whittle, *Memoirs of Bliss*, p. 235.

87 Letter to a friend, October 6, 1871, quoted in Whittle, *Memoirs of Bliss*, p. 255.

88 Letter to mother, February 19, 1871, quoted in Whittle, *Memoirs of Bliss*, p. 235.

89 Letter to William Jennings, December 8, 1875, quoted in Whittle, *Memoirs of Bliss*, p. 265.

90 Letter to William Jennings, March 24, 1876, quoted in Whittle, *Memoirs of Bliss*, p. 268.

91 Letter, March 10, 1874, quoted in Whittle, *Memoirs of Bliss*, p. 257.

take himself too seriously.

While he could joke with his wife, he was forceful in acknowledging her significant role in his life. A pastor friend recalled Bliss's "generous and enthusiastic acknowledgment of indebtedness to his noble wife for early encouragement in his musical tastes." He remembered Bliss's telling of his wife's selling the two cows which were part of her "marriage patrimony" to help her husband pursue his musical studies.[92] "I owe everything to my wife," Bliss once told a friend.[93] "My dear wife is fully my equal as a performer and far superior in matters of taste, criticism, etc.," he stated.[94] On another occasion he wrote newlyweds that he was "married before I was twenty-one. I pity poor folks who have to wait and wait! Much valuable time is lost by waiting." And he concluded: "Only may he be as happy in married life as has been his and your loving friend and brother. P. P. Bliss."[95]

In 1874, Bliss wrote his one-time teacher, "As she [Mrs. Bliss] is not to read this, I must say she is an extraordinary woman. You don't know many women of such unselfish devotion, sublime faith, and child-like trust. She lives so near the Lord that I ought to be a good man. Humanly speaking, my life would have been a failure without her. God bless her."[96] In his diary for June 1, 1859, Bliss had documented his hopes: "Called at the Reverend Mr. Barr's in Wysox and was married, by him, to Miss Lucy J. Young; although a very important step, hope it may result in happiness to us both."[97] By all evidence, the marriage was a remarkable friendship and partnership.

Together, the Blisses provided music for the meetings with

92 The Rev. D. W. Morgan, quoted in Whittle, *Memoirs of Bliss,* p. 320.

93 Quoted in Whittle, *Memoirs of Bliss,* p. 312.

94 Letter, March 31, 1874, quoted in Whittle, *Memoirs of Bliss,* p. 257.

95 Letter to Mr. and Mrs. Crafts, June 11, 1874, Whittle, *Memoirs of Bliss,* p. 243.

96 Letter quoted in Whittle, *Memoirs of Bliss,* p. 257–258.

97 Quoted in Detty, *Centennial Sketch,* p. 11.

Whittle through the latter half of 1874 and 1875. In their last year, 1876, they spent a week with Moody at Northfield, Massachusetts, where the evangelist utilized their talents in a whirlwind of eleven meetings in various venues, a pace characteristic of Moody. Bliss learned firsthand about Moody's fast driving that inspired a riddle among locals, asking, "Why is Moody so good?" Answer: "Because he drives so fast the devil can't catch him." On one occasion en route to Greenfield, Massachusetts, Moody drove their buggy so fast that Bliss actually became sick and had to lie down and rest before he was able to sing.[98]

With Whittle, their meetings ranged from Racine and Madison, Wisconsin, to St. Louis, to Mobile, Montgomery and Selma, Alabama; Augusta, Georgia, Chicago, Kalamazoo, and Jackson, Michigan. In Alabama, for example, they met with great response. The *Mobile Register* for Friday morning, March 10, 1876, noted:

WHITTLE AND BLISS—These renowned evangelists, who are as much a sensation in the South, as Moody and Sankey are in the North, are meeting with a success in this city which far transcends that which was expected by our citizens. At Government Street Presbyterian Church nightly at half-past 7, at the St. Francis-street Methodist Church daily, at 12 M, and at the St. Francis-street Baptist Church daily, at 5 P.M., their services are numerously attended, and crowds go away from one service so much pleased and edified that they gladly come again at 5 in the afternoon and at night at half-past 7. . . . Bliss, the singer, is endowed with a voice clear, resonant and highly cultivated. Like Whittle, it shows unmistakable signs of wear and tear, but he seems at present to be suffering from the singer's bete noir—hoarseness. . . . Many shed tears, while others sob and weep violently during the singing of some of his pathetic songs. He is a tall man, of large frame, erect, graceful and dignified in his carriage. His voice, in speaking, is low and

---

98 Pollock, *Moody,* p. 218. Bliss wrote his friend, Whittle: "Just returned from a week with Bro. Moody, in his home at Northfield, driving one hundred miles over Vermont, Massachusetts and New Hampshire hills and holding eleven meetings." Later, Whittle said Bliss enjoyed being with Moody immensely, and laughed about Moody's habit of working his visitors hard (Whittle, *Memoirs of Bliss,* p. 75).

clear, and his manner easy, quiet and natural. . . . He accompanies himself on a cabinet organ, and the excellence and sweetness of his accompaniment has much to do with the effectiveness of his singing.[99]

The press commented on Bliss's singing as "peculiarly effective" and "one of the great attractions." It noted, "There is a pathos in his rendition of those simple little sacred songs that touches a sympathetic chord in the breast of every one present." [100] On at least one occasion, Bliss's singing, culminating in "The Ninety and Nine," evoked a surprising round of applause that had to be quenched by Whittle.[101] When, after ten days, the duo left the city of Mobile, the newspaper reported that their farewell meeting gathered the largest crowd ever assembled in a Mobile church, and that "not only every seat, but every square foot of space in the aisles, in the galleries, upon the stairs and in the vestibules was occupied, and hundreds were compelled to go away without being able to get so far as the top step looking to the vestibule." [102]

Whittle and Bliss continued on to Montgomery and Selma. Again, great crowds thronged their meetings. In his *Memoirs of Philip P. Bliss,* Whittle made a poignant comment about what must have been a surprising special effort, all the more admirable now, realizing they were meeting only a little more than a decade after the Civil War: "Here [Montgomery], as in Mobile, special pains were taken to hold services for the colored people, and arrangements made for their attending the general meetings." [103]

The evangelistic team of Whittle and Bliss must have felt highly fulfilled as the year 1876 was drawing to a close with

---

99 "City Intelligence," *The Mobile Register,* March 10, 1876, p. 1.

100 "City Intelligence," *The Mobile Register,* March 9, 1876, p. 1.

101 "City Intelligence," *The Mobile Register,* March 14, 1876, p. 1.

102 "Messrs. Whittle and Bliss," *The Mobile Register,* March 18, 1876, p. 1.

103 Whittle, *Memoirs of Bliss,* p. 67.

services in Peoria, concluding December 14. From Peoria at the end of November, Bliss had written his friend James McGranahan, wishing him "a merry Thanksgiving and a Happy '77." [104] He had even turned to Whittle and asked, "Who is there that McGranahan could go with to sing the Gospel?" But they could not think of anyone.

There had been talk of the two Blisses and Whittle coming to Chicago to relieve Moody and Sankey at the end of December and to carry on the ministry while the latter two were in Boston and the East during the early part of the New Year. Then, it was hoped that all would go to Britain, for a return visit of Moody and Sankey, who had been so astonishingly effective there, and where Bliss's songs were beloved, especially "Jesus Loves Even Me," which had been so instantly popular. (As Sankey noted, "more than any other hymn, it became the keynote of meetings there," [105] with "Hold the Fort!" a close second.[106])

The general plan that evolved was for the Blisses to be with family in Rome (Pennsylvania) for the holidays, going on to Chicago December 31 to sing at Chicago Avenue Church, commonly called "Mr. Moody's church," (now known as Moody Memorial Church, Chicago). Moody and Sankey had been holding extra services there in response to popular demand and had grown weary. Moody, especially, was looking forward to the relief Whittle and Bliss would afford. Yet, Bliss seemed strangely reluctant about helping in Chicago after Christmas. Whittle observed that "Mr. Bliss from the very first, had an almost unaccountable aversion to the plan proposed of his returning

---

104 Whittle, *Memoirs of Bliss,* p. 250.

105 Sankey, *Sankey's Story,* p. 129; Whittle, *Memoirs of Bliss,* p. 169.

106 Bliss once told Sankey that he hoped he would not be known to posterity only as the author of "Hold the Fort!," since he believed he had written many better songs. However, Lord Shaftesbury said at the conclusion of the 1873–74 Moody–Sankey meetings in London, "If Mr. Sankey has done no more than teach the people to sing 'Hold the Fort!,' he has conferred an inestimable blessing on the British empire" (Sankey, *Sankey's Story,* p. 102; Whittle, *Memoirs of Bliss,* p. 335). Moody thought "Free from the Law" would live always (Whittle, *Memoirs of Bliss,* p. 311).

from his Christmas visit to his children, to Chicago and work there." [107] As early as December 4, after talking things over with Bliss, Whittle had written in his diary, "We had rather go anywhere else than to Chicago, and shrink much from following Mr. Moody there." [108] Just before leaving Peoria to go their respective ways for Christmas, Whittle noted, "Bliss yielded about coming to Chicago, but to the last was unconvinced as to its being best." [109]

When the two parted, they agreed that the Blisses would come to Chicago, only provided Whittle sent a definite, confirming word over the holidays. Wednesday, the 27th, only two days before his tragic death, Bliss's letter came to Whittle, stating, "I hear nothing from you definite as to my being wanted in Chicago next Sunday. Unless I hear from you, I shall not leave this week." [110] Since Bliss had been advertised as singing at Moody's church the following Sunday, December 31, Whittle knew he had to send a telegram to Bliss: yet, putting it off until the last, he explained that he did not forget to send it, "but did not want to send it." "I did not know then, I do not know now, why." Finally, late in the evening, the telegram was sent. [111]

In that strange way in which tragedies sometimes bring forth retrospective awareness of a foreboding or premonition, Whittle remembered that while in their meetings in Peoria, during their daily walks, he and Bliss had spoken of the time possibly nearing when one of them might be "walking alone, and thinking of the departed one in places where we had been together." They had also solemnly recalled the sudden death of their friend, Samuel Moody, D. L.'s older brother. [112]

---

107 Whittle, *Memoirs of Bliss*, p. 86.

108 Ibid., p. 86.

109 Ibid., p. 91.

110 Ibid., pp. 92–93.

111 Ibid.

112 Ibid, p. 90.

The unknown future before them, back in Rome, the old hometown, they spent "the happiest Christmas he had ever known" with his mother, sister, and in-laws. "Phil," as the family and locals always called him, had played the part of Santa Claus, had cut down their Christmas tree, arranged it in the parlor, and hung on the tree his own surprises, gifts they had been making and purchasing for weeks. Wednesday, the 27th, Bliss conducted a special meeting, singing many of his songs with gravity and impressiveness. Thursday morning, he called his two boys aside and had farewell prayer with them, said his goodbyes to all the family, and left the children in the care of Mrs. Bliss's sister, Clara. They checked their luggage through to Chicago and boarded the train at Waverly, New York, expecting to be in Buffalo at midnight. But an engine broke down twenty miles from Waverly. Unable to make their planned connection, they left that train at Hornellsville, New York, probably in hopes of a good night's rest. Whittle found their names as registered guests at the Osborne House there. The Blisses then connected with the ill-fated train, departed Buffalo, Friday at noon, their trunk having gone on ahead of them.[113]

From Buffalo, the train puffed its way through the snowy silence, just after seven the evening of December 29, 1876, Bliss was observed in a parlor car with work spread out in his lap. Whittle knew he had recently completed verses he titled, "My Redeemer," and "I've Passed the Cross of Calvary."[114] To the latter words, over the holidays he had come up with a fitting tune that he sang with much feeling to the gathered family and, intending to work on it aboard the train, had placed it in his satchel for further attention. It may have been the very piece that occupied him as the train plowed through the snow. Crossing a trestle about a hundred yards from the station at Ashtabula,

---

113 Ibid., p. 324; p. 93. Peet even learned from some source that Bliss sought to change his ticket and take an alternate route, but acquiesced when his originally scheduled train suddenly appeared (Peet, p. 21).

114 Whittle, *Memoirs of Bliss*, p. 61.

Ohio, passengers heard a terrible cracking sound. In just seconds, the trestle fractured, and the train plunged seventy feet into the shallow water of a deep gulf, the lead engine having made it across, but, after a momentary pause, the rest of the train fell into eternity, its wooden cars erupting in hellish flames fed by heating stoves. Approximately, one hundred passengers were killed or died later of injuries sustained in the crash, and approximately seventy were injured. It was the worst railroad tragedy to that point in American history, and one of the worst bridge disasters in America.[115]

A story that circulated at the time, probably originated with J. E. Burchell, a surviving passenger, whose business associate, B. F. Jacobs, was a supporter of D. L. Moody's work in Chicago. In his account of the accident, Burchell, helped to rescue one lady passenger, Mrs. Bingham, whom he carried with great effort up the snowy hillside to an engine house, and exhausted, did not go back. However, though he never returned to the wreckage and, thus, could not have actually observed the incident, he told the following story.

> When the train fell, Mr. Bliss succeeded in crawling through a window, supposing he could pull his wife and children after him. But they were jammed fast and every effort of his was unavailing. The car was all jammed up, and the lady and her children were caught in the ironwork of the seats. Finding that he could not save them, he staid there with them and died.[116]

The touching anecdote was picked up by newspapers and others and became a part of the tragedy's lore. In fact, there was

---

115 Of all the commentary on the bridge failure and its causes, the most preposterous historical account I have found is in a volume published by the Railroad in the Collection of Ashtabula's Hubbard House–Underground Railroad Museum, *Lake Shore and Michigan Southern Railway System and Representative Employees*, (Buffalo, NY: Biographical Publishing Company, 1900). It states: "On December 29, 1876, the valley of Ashtabula Creek, a little east of Ashtabula, was swept by a hurricane rushing onward at sixty miles an hour. The iron bridge across the creek succumbed to the fearful blast. At that moment, 7:28 p.m., amid the intense darkness and cold, the Pacific Express train, west bound, reached the smitten structure and was hurled into the chasm below" (pp. 65–66).

116 Quoted in Whittle, *Memoirs of Bliss*, p. 295.

a persistent story, corroborated by several different witnesses, and so, having the ring of truth, of a father perishing in the attempt to save his wife and children. Yet, Bliss's children were not on the train, and it seems likely that, in a case of mistaken identity, with its retelling, the incident came to involve Bliss.

Whittle discussed the story at the funeral service for the Blisses at Rome, January 7, 1877, nine days after the accident. He quoted Burchell's story, which he labeled, Burchell's "conjecture," and about which he declared, "I cannot find that this is true."[117]As one of the pastors stated in a memorial service for Bliss, the story of his returning to the fire to rescue his wife would be "just like his tender, generous, manly nature: but we do not know."[118]

As a check on the credibility of the story making the rounds, Whittle, who was on the scene in Ashtabula approximately forty-three hours after the accident,[119] passed around among survivors a picture of Bliss. He found only one lady who recognized him.[120] It seems very possible that the actual story could involve the Charles Brunner family of Bethlehem, Pennsylvania, which included a man and wife and two children, all lost with no identifiable remains, save Mr. Brunner's damaged watch, which was recovered and claimed.[121] The Brunners and the Martins (mentioned previously as the family moving to a farm near Ashtabula, and the wife having birthed a child the morning after the accident) were the only

---

117 Whittle, *Memoirs of Bliss,* p. 324.

118 Rev. N. D. Williamson of South Bend, IN in Whittle, *Memoirs of Bliss,* p. 351.

119 Whittle, p. 303, 342. The great heart and compassion of Moody are demonstrated in the immediate dispatch of John Farwell, B. F. Jacobs, Whittle, and others to Ashtabula to verify the report and claim remains for burial. Farwell was a wealthy retail merchant, grand supporter, and friend of Moody, and one who enjoyed Moody's fullest confidence.

120 Rev. N. D. Williamson of South Bend, IN, in Whittle, *Memoirs of Bliss,* p. 351.

121 Letters from Charles Brunner's father, Samuel Brunner, to E. W. Richards, and from E. W. Richards, acting coroner, to Samuel Brunner are part of the collection of letters in the Jennie Munger Gregory Memorial Museum, Geneva-on-the-Lake, Ohio.

two complete families (mother, father, two children) aboard the train at the time, and only the Martins survived.

Not a trace of P. P. or Lucy Bliss was ever found, not an artifact or possession. Contemporaries noted it was as though he was taken up "in a chariot of fire." So beloved was the young couple that special memorial services were held in Chicago, in Rome (Pennsylvania), at South Bend, St. Paul, Louisville, Nashville, Kalamazoo, and Peoria. The great monument in the little cemetery at Rome was dedicated with a large crowd and with Moody, Sankey, Whittle and many dignitaries present, the day after what would have been Bliss's thirty-ninth birthday, July 10, 1877. A cenotaph in Ashtabula's Chestnut Grove Cemetery, erected nearly nineteen years after the accident, memorializes all those "unidentified" who perished in the Ashtabula Railroad disaster, including "P. P. Bliss and wife."

Bliss's trunk had been checked through to Chicago, and in it, were a number of written pieces, all seeming especially prescient, having survived his fiery end. One was a little verse that became very familiar to Whittle and Bliss after first repeated in Kalamazoo:

> In peace I go; no fear I know
> Since Christ walks by my side.
> His love to me my joy shall be,
> His words shall be my guide.[122]

Another set of words was "My Redeemer," destined to become popular after Bliss's friend James McGranahan added a joyful melody. It was McGranahan for whom Bliss had yearned to find an evangelistic partner just one month previously, and McGranahan who took his place as Major Whittle's musical associate.

Also among his papers in the checked trunk was a manuscript including music, entitled "He Knows." Originally, it was suspected of being Bliss's own, but actually represented an adaptation of the words of Mary G. Brainard (1837–1905), a

---

122 Whittle, *Memoirs of Bliss*, p. 78.

contemporary poet, words so especially poignant after Bliss's death. "He Knows" was sung as the closing hymn at the Blisses' funeral, after Whittle told the assembled crowd, "had Mr. Bliss desired to leave a special message of comfort to his bereaved friends, appropriate to their present calamity, he could not have left anything more beautiful or more comforting." [123]

> I know not what awaits me,
> God kindly veils my eyes,
> And o'er each step of my onward way
> He makes new scenes to rise;
> And ev'ry joy He sends me comes
> A sweet and glad surprise.
> So on I go, not knowing,
> I would not if I might;
> I'd rather walk in the dark with God
> Than go alone in the light;
> I'd rather walk by faith with Him,
> Than go alone by sight. [124]

Even more touching, perhaps, is the text of yet another leaflet, author unknown, found in Bliss's surviving trunk. Whittle recognized it as a paper he had carried with him a long time in his pocketbook, as though planning to put it to some specific use, until creased and worn, he simply placed it with other papers.

---

123 Quoted in Whittle, *Memoirs of Bliss*, p. 339.

124 Whittle, *Memoirs of Bliss*, p. 64, incorrectly attributes the poem to Alice Carey (1820–1871), a sentimental poet who, as was not uncommon in the Victorian era, wrote a great deal about death. I found Mary Gardiner Brainard's complete poem, entitled "Not Knowing," and attributed only to "Congregationalist" (presumably, the publication from which it had been gleaned), in *Friends' Review*, August 28, 1869, p. 15.

A VOICE FROM HEAVEN [125]

I shine in the light of God,	Rev. xxi.23.
His likeness stamps my brow,	I John iii.2.
Through the shadows of death my feet have trod,	I Cor. xv.55
And I reign in Glory now!	Rev. xxii.5
No breaking heart is here,	Matt. xxvi.38
No keen and thrilling pain,	Job xxxiii.19
No wasted cheek, where the frequent tear	Rev. xxi.4
Hath roll'd and left its stain.	Ps. xlii.3
I have found the joys of Heaven,	Is. xxxv.10
I am one of the angel-band:	Heb. xii.22
To my head a crown of gold is given,	I Pet. v.4
And a harp is in my hand!	Rev. xiv.2
I have learn'd the song they sing	Is. xxxviii.20
Whom Jesus hath set free:	John viii.36
And the glorious walls of Heaven still ring	Is. lx.18
With my new-born melody!	Rev. xv.8
No sin, no grief, no pain —	Is. xxv.8
Safe in my happy home!	John xiv.2
My fears all fled, my doubts all slain,	Acts vii.55
My hour of triumph come!	Rom. viii.37
O friends of mortal years,	Prov. xvii.17
The trusted and the true!	I John i.7
Ye are walking still through the valley of tears,	Heb. x.36
But I wait to welcome you.	Luke xvi.22
Do I forget?—Oh no!	Mal. iii.16
For memory's golden chain	2 Pet. i.15
Shall bind my heart to the hearts below,	I John iv.7
Till they meet and touch again.	I Thess. iv.13
Each link is strong and bright,	John i.51
And love's electric flame	Dan. ix.21
Flows freely down like a river of light	Rev. xxii.1
To the world from which I came.	I John iv.9
Do you mourn when another star	I Cor. xv.41
Shines out from the glittering sky?	Dan. xii.3
Do you weep when the raging voice of war	Deut. xxxii.1
And the storms of conflict die?	Mark iv.39
Then why do your tears run down,	Luke viii.52
And your hearts be sorely riven,	Prov. xiv.10
For another gem in the Savior's crown,	Is.lxii.3
And another soul in Heaven?	Luke xxiii.43

—Anonymous

---

125 Quoted in Whittle, *Memoirs of Bliss,* pp. 95–96.

It is part of the human condition that we do not control our own destinies, the numbering of the days of our lives. So, like all the victims of the Ashtabula train-bridge tragedy, Bliss left this life with unfinished work, on his schedule, in his mind, in his trunk, and in his satchel—melodies without words, words without melodies. Back in Pennsylvania, he and his wife left two small boys who would never really know their parents.[126] Their musician friend Ira D. Sankey was left in a hotel in Chicago waiting that Saturday morning, December 30, 1876, to greet the Blisses upon arrival and to enjoy their company. R. C. Morgan, publisher and British church leader, had returned to Chicago early from Canada hoping to convince the Blisses to come to England the following spring.[127] From the perspective of 125 years, we understand D. L. Moody's text, Sunday, following the disaster: "Therefore be ye also ready" (Matthew 24.44).[128]

---

126 Philip Paul Bliss, born November 25, 1872, became a published composer of sacred and secular music. He composed about two hundred piano pieces, operettas, cantatas, choruses, and songs before his death in Owego, New York, February 2, 1933, at age sixty He is buried in Owego. Married to the former Lina Mayor of Owego; they had no children. George Goodwin Bliss, born August 27, 1874, was graduated from Princeton University and became an auditor and accountant. He died at age fifty-nine, in Candor, New York, December 29, 1933, the 57th anniversary of his young parents' deaths in the Ashtabula railway-bridge accident, and is buried at Candor. George was married to the former May Belcher, who died in Binghamton, New York, January 12, 1940. They had no children (Neil, pp 29–31; Detty, p. 35). The two boys grew up with Mr. and Mrs. John S. Ellsworth (Mrs. Bliss's sister, Clara), and the Ellsworths' son, Charles (Detty, p. 35). Although there is scant mention of it, the Blisses apparently lost a child before the births of their two sons identified here (letter from The Reverend Darwin Cook, quoted in Whittle, *Memoirs of Bliss,* p. 25.)

127 Charles Ludwig, *Sankey Still Sings* (Anderson, IN, 1947) p. 109; Whittle, *Memoirs of Bliss,* p. 303.

128 Whittle, *Memoirs of Bliss,* pp. 345–347.

Sources Consulted

Adams, Jr., Charles Francis. *Notes on Railroad Accidents.* New York, 1879.

The Alabama Baptist. 1876.

The Ashtabula Bridge Disaster Collection of Original Letters and Papers. The Jennie Munger Gregory Memorial Museum, Geneva-on-the-Lake, Ohio.

Ashtabula News. 1877.

Ashtabula Sentinel. 1877.

Ashtabula Telegraph. 1877.

"Bliss, Philip Paul," in *Appleton's Cyclopaedia of American Biography.* 2 vols., New York, 1887.

Bliss, P. P. "Hold the Fort!" Boston, 1877.

P. P. Bliss Gospel Songwriters Museum. Rome, Pennsylvania

Crafts, Mrs. W. F. (Sara J. Timanus). "Biographical Sketch of P. P. Bliss," in *Song Victories of the 'Bliss and Sankey Hymns.'* Dover, New Hampshire, 1877.

Detty, Victor C. *P. P. Bliss July 9, 1838—December 29, 1876: A Centennial Sketch of His Life and Work 1838–1938 with Selected Gospel Hymns.* Wysox, Pennsylvania. 1938.

Dorsett, Lyle W. *The Life of D. L. Moody: A Passion for Souls.* Chicago, 1997.

Friends' Review. August 28, 1869.

Goff, Jr., James R. *Close Harmony: A History of Southern Gospel.* Chapel Hill, 2002.

Goodspeed, E. J. *A Full History of the Wonderful Career of Moody and Sankey, in Great Britain and America.* New York, 1876.

Griswold, Wesley S. *Train Wreck!* Brattleboro, VT, 1969.

The Hubbard House–Underground Railroad Museum, Ashtabula, Ohio

Lake Shore and Michigan Southern Railway System and Representative Employees. Buffalo, New York, 1900

Ludwig, Charles. *Sankey Still Sings.* Anderson, Indiana, 1947.

The Mobile Register. 1876.

Moody, William. *The Life of Dwight L. Moody.* New York, 1900.

Neil, Bobby Joe. "Philip P. Bliss (1838–1876): Gospel Hymn Composer and Compiler." Unpublished dissertation, New Orleans Baptist Theological Seminary, 1977.

Peet, Stephen D. *The Ashtabula Disaster.* Chicago, 1877.

Pollock, John C. *Moody: A Biographical Portrait of the Pacesetter in Modern Mass Evangelism.* New York, 1963.

Pollock, John C. *Moody without Sankey.* London, 1963.

Sankey, Ira D. *Sankey's Story of the Gospel Hymns.* Philadelphia, 1906.

Scheips, Paul J. *Hold the Fort! The Story of a Song from the Sawdust Trail to the Picket Line.* Washington, 1971.

Scigliano, Eric. "10 Technology Disasters." *Technology Review,* 105:48–52, (June) 2002.

Simons, M. Laird. *Holding the Fort: Comprising Sermons and Addresses at the Great Revival Meetings Conducted by Moody and Sankey; With Proceedings of Christian Convention of Ministers and Laymen, and Also the Lives and Labors of Dwight L. Moody, Ira D. Sankey, and P. P. Bliss.* Philadelphia, 1877.

Smith, Henry Nash ed. *Popular Culture and Industrialism, 1865–1890.* New York, 1967.

Smucker, David. "Philip Paul Bliss and the Musical, Cultural and Religious Sources of the Gospel Music Tradition in the United States, 1850–1876." Unpublished dissertation, Boston University, 1981.

Stevenson, Robert. *Protestant Church Music in America: A Short Survey of Men and Movements from 1564 to the Present.* New York, 1966.

The Terrible Ashtabula Railroad Calamity, on the Evening of Dec. 29th 1876, Together with a Few Incidents of P. P. Bliss, the Immortal Singer. Perkasie, Pa., n.d.

Whittle, Daniel W. ed. *Memoirs of Philip P. Bliss.* New York, 1877.

The Ashtabula Horror
Charles A. Burnham

A native of Ashtabula, Charles Burnham is the founder of the Ashtabula Railway Historical Foundation. His interest in the bridge disaster began with a high school term paper and has continued throughout his life as a research and developmental engineer. He conducts tours of the site, and serves on the Beacon Production advisory team to create a documentary of the disaster.

The bridge was the crucial element in the "Ashtabula Horror" and became the subject of endless speculation. Over the years, investigatory panels, professional engineers, and amateur train enthusiasts have pondered the train, the cold, the snow, the weaknesses of the bridge, and wondered why it fell.

The Ashtabula River bridge, known then as the Ashtabula Creek bridge, which fell apart the night of December 29, 1876, was a replacement for a wooden Howe truss bridge that previously occupied the site. Erected eleven years earlier, the new structure was designed by the president of the Cleveland, Painesville, and Ashtabula Railroad, Amasa Stone, a partner with his brother-in-law, Elias Howe, in the Howe Bridge and Truss Company (Reed, 1968).

Stone, an expert in wooden bridges, designed for Ashtabula an innovative span built of iron. It happened that Stone's brother, Andros B. Stone, was a partner in the Cleveland iron works chosen to provide the I-beams for the bridge's superstructure. Stone hired Joseph Tomlinson to develop design specifications for the individual bridge members, to draw up detailed shop drawings for fabrication, and to supervise construction. As a civil engineer who had done contract bridge building since 1846, Tomlinson was well-qualified. The design

Stone handed off to Tomlinson placed the superstructure, consisting of two iron Howe trusses, below track level, the bridge's deck to rest directly on the upper chord, and the tracks to be placed so that a train would load ninety percent of one truss and only ten percent of the other. Tomlinson's specifications, called for a six-inch camber in the bridge's upper chord or deck. (Camber is a slight upward arch in the bridge deck, which tends to flatten out when bearing a load).

The main diagonal bracing would be I-beams 260-inches long, six-inches high, and with flanges four-inches wide. This bracing would interlock into lugs on angle blocks in the bridge's upper chord and attach to tensioning braces forming the lower chord. The bridge's upper chord consisted of segments, which were two panels long, and with the same angle blocks, the diagonal braces were set (Gasparini and Fields, 1993). One specification issued by Stone was to proportion the structure such that it would bear eight thousand pounds per square inch in tension and eight thousand pounds per square inch in compression. The specification for the compression elements was a source of conflict between Stone and Tomlinson, since Tomlinson figured eight thousand pounds per square inch on the compression elements would actually bend the diagonal I-beams.

The diagonals arrived at the original construction site undersized; so, Tomlinson went to Stone with proposals to reinforce the diagonals. When Stone would not hear of any changes, Tomlinson resigned from the project (Gasparini and Fields, 1993).

Erecting the Bridge

With Tomlinson gone, Stone chose to supervise construction himself, rather than assign the task to Charles Collins, chief engineer of the railroad. Stone felt that with vast experience building wooden bridges and a few with iron, completing the Ashtabula bridge would be a crowning achievement to his career. The task of erecting the bridge was assigned to A. L. Rogers, a carpenter who built and repaired wooden bridges for the railroad, but who had never worked on an iron bridge. Rogers was likely chosen because Stone believed him to be competent, and that the bridge was to be built of iron, he considered of little or no consequence. Rogers worked with road-master mechanic Albert Congdon, a man with extensive iron experience (Gasparini and Fields, 1993).

Rogers' first task was to build the false work or temporary support upon which the bridge was to be erected. At first, with Congdon's recommendation, Rogers planned a camber in the false work of five-to-seven inches. (Such a camber concurred generally with Tomlinson's design specification of six inches.) However, Stone told Rogers that the bridge was never designed for that much camber, and that the correct value should be a half-inch to the panel. To comply, Rogers changed the camber of the false work to three-and-one-half inches. At this point the first erection problem presented itself. When a camber of three-and-one-half inches was used, instead of the six inches called for by Tomlinson, the I-beams for the upper chord were too long to fit between the angle blocks. Rogers' remedy for this was to shorten the members of the upper chord of each truss.

After the correction was completed, the final task was to "screw up" vertical rods to pre-stress each truss. When Rogers began to remove the false work, due to the shortened chords, the bridge deflected or yielded two and one-half inches below the horizontal. Considering the deflection, removal of the false work was halted for fear the bridge might fall. To remedy the problem, Stone ordered the upper chords returned to their original lengths using shims. The shims fit because Rogers reportedly changed the bridge camber back to six inches, as originally specified by Tomlinson. The bridge was then pre-stressed with the vertical adjustment rods before a second attempt at removing the supporting false work. However, inadvertently, some diagonals were pre-stressed to the buckling

"The bridge was very high, and loomed up in the distance, tall and dark and gloomy. Travelers by the wagon road, at a distance up the river a mile away, would stop and look at this structure, . . . and watch the cars as they passed in bold relief against the sky. . . . There was something almost fearful in the sight. The recklessness of danger impressed the observer. . . . Here, then, was the bridge. . . , a mysterious thing." (Stephen D. Peet, *The Ashtabula Disaster*, 1877, p. 14) *(Photo from Jennie Munger Gregory Memorial Museum Collection.)*

With the iron bridge reduced to a pile of incinerated rubble, the stark grandeur of the great stone arches, rising seventy-six feet above the gulf floor, is clearly evident against the winter sky. *(Blakeslee & Moore photo courtesy of the Jennie Munger Gregory Memorial Museum.)*

The 32-ton locomotive, Socrates, with its prominent smokestack, lantern, and cowcatcher (pilot), made it across, thanks to the quick-witted action of veteran engineer Dan McGuire. Note that the tender is off the track, thrown up against the cab. *(Blakeslee & Moore photo courtesy of the Jennie Munger Gregory Memorial Museum Collection.)*

Looking east to west, toward the station, the stone abutment stands as a surviving remnant of the bridge. The wooden stairs are visible at an angle slanting down the embankment. Note bystanders in foreground. *(Blakeslee & Moore photo courtesy of the Jennie Munger Gregory Memorial Museum Collection.)*

A close-up of the wreckage, at the base of the west abutment, showing the Columbia in clearer detail. Note how little (and largely metal) remains of the railcars, the unintended funeral pyre for an unknown number of victims. *(Blakeslee & Moore photo courtesy of David Tobias.)*

The fallen locomotive, the Columbia, was one of the few elements of the wreckage clearly identifiable after the fire. The view faces north. After failed attempts, it was brought up the gulf, put on track, and hauled away for repairs. *(Blakeslee & Moore photo courtesy of the Jennie Munger Gregory Memorial Museum Collection.)*

The stone bridge abutment, looking west to east, the morning after the tragedy, the fire only smoldering. In the foreground, several workers are visible removing the dead. According to the *Ashtabula News* (January 10, 1877), Blakeslee and Moore were on the scene at 6 a.m. the morning after, and took the only photographs of the accident, eleven different perspectives. Blakeslee, a volunteer fireman, had been present the previous evening assisting with the rescue. *(Blakeslee & Moore photo courtesy of the Jennie Munger Gregory Memorial Museum Collection.)*

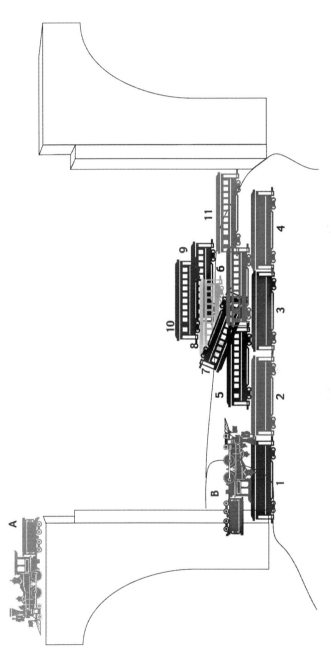

Schematic of the accident. Bridge fell to the north. Train was on the south track westbound. The actual railroad tracks fell straight down.
A = Socrates engine made it across, B = Columbia engine fell on top of first express car (#1)
1 = Express car, 2 = Express car, 3 = Baggage car, 4 = Baggage car, 5 = First passenger coach, 6 = Second passenger coach, 7 = Smoker, 8 = Yokahama drawing-room car or parlor car, 9 = Palatine sleeper, 10 = City of Buffalo sleeper (up in the air possibly leaning against pier), 11 = Osceo sleeper. (*Graphic by Larry Hunter, according to David Tobias.*)

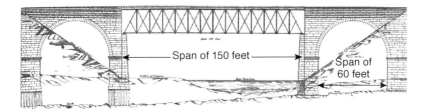

When built in 1863, the Ashtabula Bridge was considered highly innovative, an iron Howe truss structure. Some people thought it was intended to be the consummate achievement of Amasa Stone, president of the Cleveland and Erie Railroad, which built the bridge before merger into the Lake Shore and Michigan Southern Railway. *(Drawing courtesy of personal collection of David Tobias.)*

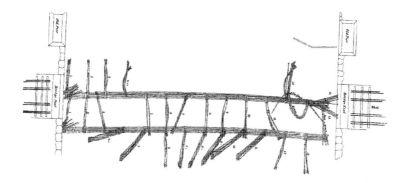

After its collapse, the postmortem on the bridge included a drawing of the way the metal was splayed in all directions, as observed three weeks after the disaster. This view is as if looking directly down from overhead. *(Drawing accompanied Report of Albert H. Howland, Civ. Eng., Boston; courtesy of personal collection of David Tobias.)*

The bridge as it has been since 1904, a double-arch design, appearing almost as two giant culverts. The railroad brought in a considerable amount of fill, greatly reducing the necessary height of the bridge and made it wide enough for four sets of tracks. *(Above)* Photo from a postcard. *(Below)* Bridge today. *(Below photo by the Reverend Virgil V. Reeve.)*

Bliss and Tragedy

P. P. Bliss had sold millions of hymnbooks and pieces of sheet music by the time of his death at age thirty-eight. One of his most popular songs, whose title became a colloquial expression, was "Hold the Fort!" sung around the world and adapted for many different uses. It was never popular in the South, since it was based on a Union Army experience. *(From editor's personal collection.)*

Philip Paul Bliss (July 9, 1838–December 29, 1876) was a world-renowned songwriter, whose works had been translated into many languages and sung all over the world even before his death at age thirty-eight. His songs are still in contemporary Protestant hymnals today. Tall, handsome, and commanding in appearance, he had a warm, humble spirit that made him beloved among all he met.

Lucy Young Bliss (March 14, 1841–December 29, 1876) was the oldest of six children of a successful Pennsylvania farmer, choirmaster of the local Presbyterian church. It is believed that Lucy Bliss taught Philip to play the organ. She was a great complement to him in musical ability and temperament. P. P. Bliss often commented gratefully on her significant role in their life together. *(Photos from editor's personal collection.)*

Fred Blakeslee took this photo soon after the monument "to the unrecognized dead" was erected in Ashtabula's Chestnut Grove Cemetery, Memorial Day, 1895. A drive for funds was begun in 1892 at the suggestion of Thomas W. McCreary, manager of the Hotel James. Among early contributors were President William H. McKinley and Mrs. James A. Garfield. James L. Smith chaired the committee, which included McCreary, Clarence E. Richardson, Lucien Seymour, and Norris W. Simons. Some funds were provided by the Knights of Pythias. The cenotaph stands thirty-five feet tall. *(Blakeslee & Moore photo courtesy of David Tobias.)*

The Chestnut Grove Cemetery monument to those never identified was erected in 1895. On January 19, 1877, the remains of forty unknown and/or unidentifiable passengers were placed in nineteen coffins and buried at the site. A few days later, four additional boxes containing unidentifiable body parts and scraps of clothing were also interred at the site. Numerous memorial observances have taken place at the site over the years, including August 3, 2002. *(Photo by the Reverend Virgil V. Reeve.)*

The Protection Fire Co. was one of the volunteer units many felt should have been employed in putting out the fire that erupted in the accident. This photograph was taken in front of the Prospect Road residence that became a funeral home, replaced by a modern structure. *(Photo courtesy of John Paul and the Ashtabula Fire Department.)*

A steamer, on the order of the one pictured here, responded to the ringing of the bell, December 29, 1876. Though on site, with sufficient manpower, the steamer was never used to put out the fire, apparently due to confusion, miscommunication, and uncertain leadership. *(Photo courtesy of John Paul and the Ashtabula Fire Department.)*

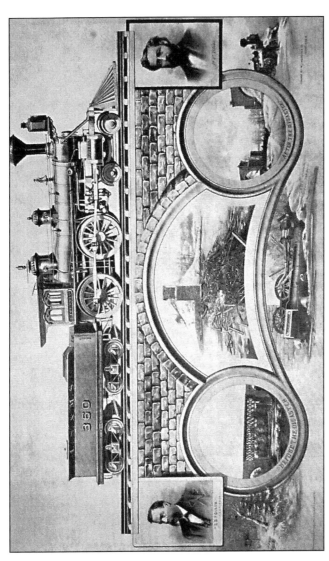

The magnitude of the accident, and the tragic deaths of Gospel songwriter, P. P. Bliss and wife, Lucy Young Bliss, made Ashtabula a household word. Clever designers came up with memorial tributes to catch the public's eye. This one was drawn by W. J. Morgan Co. of Cleveland, and printed in 1882. The copyright was held by by G. D. Folsom and S. C. King, of St. Louis, Missouri, and includes the photographs, pre- and post-accident, by Blakeslee & Moore. G. D. "Pap" Folsom, of Cleveland, was the engineer who survived, though his Columbia fell to the floor of the gulf below. Folsom's being one of the copyright holders may explain the prominence of his photograph opposite Bliss's. *(Photo courtesy of the Hubbard House–UGRR Museum.)*

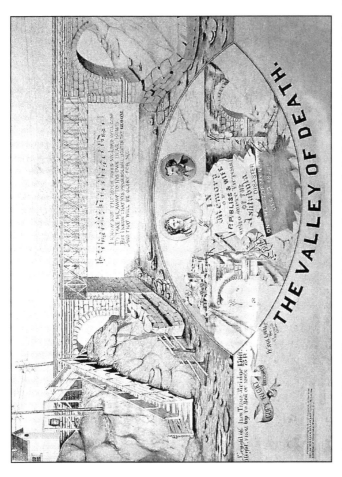

Another souvenir lithograph is entitled "The Valley of Death." It depicts the Ashtabula Bridge, both before and after the accident, and shows the steps leading down the western side (station side) of the gulf. Designed by William Sullivant, of Gustavus, Ohio, it includes the engine Socrates, portraits of P. P. and Lucy Young Bliss, and the words from a verse of the Bliss hymn, "That Will Be Heaven For Me." According to the *Ashtabula News* (February 21,1877), it was printed on card stock, 14 x 17 inches and sold for one dollar. *(Photo courtesy of the Hubbard House–UGRR Museum.)*

A book, *Helen's Babies,* was among unclaimed articles listed for public sale at a price of ten cents. The description notes that it was wrapped in brown paper, but that it was burned. *(Courtesy of Hubbard House–UGRR Museum.)*

An unclaimed valise survived the fire, without contents or a name. Mrs. Sims of E. 44th Street said that it had been handed down among members of her family since the time of the disaster. She gave it to the late Charles Moses in the summer of 1987. *(Courtesy of Hubbard House–UGRR Museum.)*

A stencil nameplate of Charles Collins, the railroad's chief bridge executive, was found in the 1980s at the site. Collins, a much-admired citizen in Ashtabula and in Cleveland, was thought to have committed suicide after the accident, but, in the opinion of medical examiners, he was murdered. *(Personal Collection of David Tobias.)*

Cuspidor from one of the wrecked train coaches was found at the site of the disaster by a boy, William Coode, who was born and raised in a house at the corner of Station Avenue and Depot Street. He later gave it to Bud Graham,

whose son, Chris, of Skokie, Illinois, donated it to Hubbard House. *(Courtesy of Hubbard House–UGRR Museum.)*

A cracked glass chimney globe from a lamp on board the train. "L-S-&-M-S-R" are clearly visible. *(Courtesy of Hubbard House–UGRR Museum.)*

Bliss and Tragedy

A silver cup was apparently a gift from Foster E. Swift to Thomas B. Tuller, proprietor of Tuller House, a hotel in Geneva, in appreciation of kindness and hospitality during recovery from the wreck. The inscription reads:

"Memento of the Ashtabula
R. R. Bridge Disaster
F. E. Swift, North Adams, Mass.
T. B. Tuller, Geneva, O.
Dec. 29th, 1876."

David Tobias believes Tuller House is still standing off North Broadway on Woodlawn in Geneva. *(Courtesy of the personal collection of David Tobias.)*

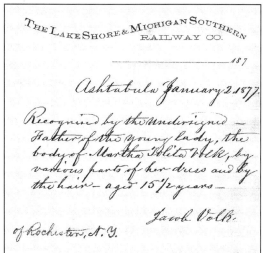

A family member or representative had to sign a release when claiming an individual's remains. To write such a receipt would have to be one of the hardest duties of fatherhood:

"Ashtabula January 2, 1877

Recognized by the undersigned Father of the young lady, the body of Martha Tolita Volk, by various parts of her dress and by the hair—aged 15 ½ years—
Jacob Volk.
of Rochester, N. Y."

(Courtesy of Jennie Munger Gregory Memorial Museum.)

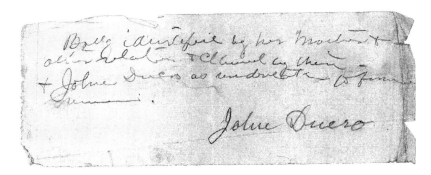

"Body identified by her mother & other relatives & claimed by them & John Ducro as undertaker to forward remains. John Ducro" Receipt is for the body of Annie Kitterville [or Ketlerville or Ketterwall] of Beloit, Wisconsin. The Ducro Family has operated a funeral business in Ashtabula for many years. Family members say they had always understood that their ancestors had been involved with the bridge disaster, but never had evidence. This receipt is in the Jennie Munger Gregory Memorial Museum. *(Courtesy of Jennie Munger Gregory Memorial Museum.)*

As late as two-and-a-half weeks after the accident, body parts were still found. This note reads: "January 17, 1877—Went down to the Depot and viewed the remains of part of a body found in the debris this day—viz: the lower part of the backbone and some of the intestines—all burnt to a crisp and brought them to the undertaker for burial. E. W. Richards. Acting Coroner" Richards appears to have been among those unsung heroes, who were placed under great physical and mental strain, but who maintained a caring spirit and dispatched duties with sincere tenderness. *(Courtesy of Jennie Munger Gregory Memorial Museum.)*

Bliss and Tragedy

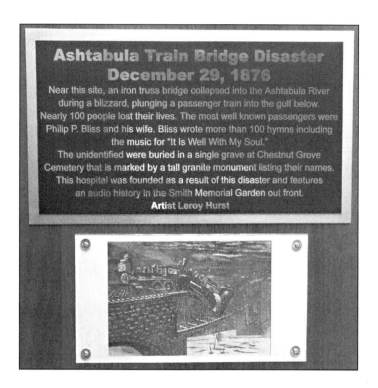

As part of the 125th-year commemoration of the accident, an audio kiosk *(below)* was dedicated in Smith Memorial Garden of Ashtabula's hospital. The 125th-year commemoration was also the inspiration for an historical marker *(above)* dedicated a year later, July 12, 2003, at the hospital, overlooking the accident site. *(Photos by the Reverend Virgil V. Reeve.)*

point; thus, proceeding with the second attempt to remove the false work, when several diagonals began to buckle, Rogers halted the process (Gasparini and Fields, 1993).

At this point, Stone ordered additional diagonal braces to reinforce the three end-panels to prevent them from buckling. It is likely that Stone reflected on Tomlinson's concerns regarding the possible buckling of the diagonals when under stress. To accommodate the additional diagonals, two modifications were made. In the first modification, lugs on the upper chord's angle blocks, which were to hold the diagonals in position, were removed to make room for the additional beams. In the second modification, ends of some diagonal braces were "chipped" away to allow clearance for the vertical iron rods. Put simply, the diagonal bracing on the three panels on each end did not have a square bearing on their respective angle blocks, and had no mechanical restraint—only friction—to hold their position. (Friction is a restraint method commonly reliable with wooden Howe trusses [Gasparini and Fields, 1993].) After these changes, Rogers made a third attempt at pre-stressing the bridge and removing the false work, and this time, the bridge stood on its own, bearing its own weight, without buckling any diagonal bracing. After a single track was laid on the bridge deck, three sixty-thousand-pound locomotives crossed in a test, and the bridge was placed in service. Later a second track was added, and many persons subsequently testified that they thought the bridge safe for one track but unable to bear two.

Two points of unknown significance should be mentioned. (1)Chief Engineer Collins never specified an optimum length of time between bridge inspections. (2)Gustavus Folsom, engineer of the Columbia, who rode his engine down with the bridge and who survived, later reported that the bridge at times "snapped" as if the joints were settling together as he crossed. Folsom also reported that although the snaps could be heard, they could not be felt.

The Locomotives and Train

At the time of the disaster, the Pacific Express, Train No. 5 on the timetable, was the "crack" New York to Chicago passenger train operated by the New York Central and Hudson River Railroad and the Lake Shore and Michigan Southern Railway (LS&MS). Historically, the term "crack" was reserved for passenger trains that were the pride of the fleet, or the "flagships." Such status was given, for example, to the New York Central's Twentieth Century Limited, of which the Pacific Express was a predecessor. The Pacific Express carried wealthy businessman of the day, wives, and children of society families, the well-known, as well as the not-so-well-known. December 29, 1876, the Pacific Express included: the lead locomotive, Socrates; the trailing locomotive, Columbia; two express cars; two baggage cars; two day coaches; a smoking car; a drawing-room car, Yokahama; the New York sleeper, Palatine; the Boston sleeper, City of Buffalo; the Louisville sleeper, Osceo (Peet, 1877).

The LS&MS Railway operated its trains in what is called "Left Handed" operation, meaning that trains traveled on the left track of a two-or-more-tracked main line. Most railroads then, as today, operate on the right-side tracks on a two-or-more tracked main line. That LS&MS operating scheme is why the Pacific Express approached Ashtabula on the south track.

The Crew

As the Pacific Express approached the Ashtabula bridge, the train crew was preparing for arrival at the Ashtabula station—the Socrates, manned by Engineer Dan McGuire and his fireman, James F. Hunt, and the Columbia, with Engineer Gustavus "Pap" Folsom and fireman Peter Livenbroe. On board the train, packages in the two express cars were being prepared to be dropped at Ashtabula by Expressmen Lawrence Lannegan, George Purington, and S. D. Waite. Baggageman Philip McNeil was organizing luggage for passengers stopping in Ashtabula, working in one of the two baggage cars. Among the passengers, Conductor Bernhart Henn and Sleeping Car Conductor Harry Wagner were in the smoking car with preparations for arrival already made. Porter James Webb worked the Yokahama, seeing to passenger concerns and preparing for the stop. In the Palatine, Porter Jerry Stewart was setting up sleeping berths for passengers continuing beyond Ashtabula. In the City of Buffalo, Porter Charles Caine (or Kane) was preparing sleeping berths and anticipating stopping. The porter of the Osceo, James Doyle, attended to the three lady occupants. Brakemen A. L. Stone and W. H. Vosburgh worked their way to the rear of the train, ready to set hand brakes at the Ashtabula station.

The Passengers

Pacific Express passengers were making the best of a journey already two-and-one-half hours late as they rolled through the snow toward the Ashtabula bridge. The first day coach with about thirty passengers included a lady sitting on the right-side front with her two-year-old nephew. A few seats behind, a young woman was reading a book. The second day coach had about forty passengers, including Ashtabula businessman George Kepler, gathering up his belongings, preparing to disembark, and thankful to be home at last after a fast trip to Erie. Sixteen passengers were in the smoking car, where LS&MS carpenter, Garwood B. Stow, was listening to a conversation among Conductor Henn, Harvey Tilden, superintendent of the LS&MS Water Works, and George M. Reed, LS&MS superintendent of bridges, concerning the weight and water consumed by the two locomotives of the train. Several passengers occupied the drawing-room car Yokahama, among them, The Reverend Dr. Alvan H. Washburn, Episcopal rector, returning home to Cleveland. In the Palatine, passengers were grouped in twos, fours, and some larger groups, eating dinner, chatting, and playing cards. Among the nineteen passengers, Marion Shepard watched the caboose from an eastbound heavy-freight train pass her window. In the City of Buffalo, Minnie Mixer, daughter of the prominent Dr. Mixer of Buffalo, New York, prepared for bed, wearing a chain from her collection of jewelry. Gospel songwriter Philip Bliss and his wife, Lucy, enjoyed each other's company and likely discussed the upcoming meetings in Chicago with evangelist D. L. Moody and Ira Sankey. Clara Thayer, nurse of Mrs. William H. Bradley, watched over Mrs. Bradley's sleeping baby, not particularly mindful of the twenty others in that car. The Osceo had only three passengers: Mrs. Frank Eastman, Mrs. W. H. Lew of Rochester, New York, and Mrs. T. A. Davis of Kokomo, Indiana (Peet, 1877).

A Night to Remember

December 29, 1876, had dawned with a "lake effect" snowstorm pelting northeast Ohio, northwest Pennsylvania, and western New York. Such "lake effect" storms were common then, as they are now, throughout the Great Lakes Region, caused typically by cold Canadian air blowing across warm lake waters. At dusk, the snow was still falling with blinding fury, and the temperature declined to sixteen degrees after a daytime high of twenty-seven. Wind velocity between Erie, Pennsylvania and Cleveland, Ohio, between 8:00 p.m. and 9:00 p.m., was reported at twenty to fifty-four miles per hour (Gasparini and Fields, 1993). In Ashtabula, roads were impassable due to drifting snow, and businesses closed early due to the storm. The station and facilities of the LS&MS Railway remained in operation. At 3:00 that afternoon, the Pacific Express departed Erie, Pennsylvania, two-and-a-half hours late, requiring the assistance of two pusher locomotives. Through the late afternoon and into the evening, engineers Dan McGuire and "Pap" Folsom ran their locomotives through what Folsom called "the worst storm he had ever experienced along the Lake Shore and Michigan Southern." (Shaw, 1961). Snowfall in Ashtabula was from twelve to thirty-six inches, depending on the severity of drifting. Not until midnight, did the snow subside to light flurries.

Collapse of the Ashtabula River Bridge

As the Pacific Express rounded the final turn to the bridge at fifteen miles per hour, through the snow, engineer Dan McGuire saw faint, blurred lights of the Ashtabula station ahead, as the train proceeded routinely onto the bridge. The time was 7:28 p.m. As the Socrates crossed the second panel point from the west abutment of the bridge, McGuire heard a sharp "crack" similar to a torpedo-signaling device, and suddenly, as he kept his eye focused forward, he had the sensation of running uphill. Instinctively, McGuire grabbed the throttle handle and pulled it wide open so that the Socrates safely reached the west abutment, severing its coupling to the Columbia. McGuire looked back with horror to see the Columbia and the rest of the train lurching wildly and seeming to hang in suspense for an instant before spilling into the gulf below.

What was actually happening, as experts later sorted out, was the coming apart of the bridge as its south truss fell away, starting at the second panel point from the west abutment. The Socrates had caused the bridge deck to lean south, causing the tender of the Socrates and the trailing Columbia to derail. Then as the north truss began to fail, a result of the leaning bridge deck, the bridge's superstructure landed in the river on the north side of the bridge. Whereupon the north truss completely failed, landing north of the bridge site, the bridge deck and track dropped straight downward, with the Columbia, both express cars, and part of the first baggage car on top of it. Eventually, it became clear that the first express car had lurched forward and landed at the foot of the west abutment, while the Columbia landed to the south side of the west abutment, slid down the bank adjacent to the abutment, and landed upside down, falling onto the first express car. The second express car and two baggage cars fell to the side of the bridge and formed a line across the ravine with the rear baggage car against the east abutment. The first passenger coach landed in an upright position in the middle of the river near the bridge wreckage. The second passenger coach struck ground at an angle and turned on its side, coming to rest atop the bridge wreckage on the north. It was crushed and broken in the fall. The smoking car struck across the second passenger coach smashing it before falling on top of the first coach, caving it in. The Yokahama, the drawing-room car, fell clear of the east abutment, ending up on the ice to the left of the bridge, eighty feet away. The sleeper Palatine landed beside the Yokahama to the right. The City of Buffalo struck the Yokahama and the Palatine in midair, knocking the Yokahama on its side, crushing it throughout its entire length. The City of Buffalo came to rest on its forward end, its rear end high in the air leaning against both the Yokahama and the Palatine. The sleeper Osceo ended up near the Palatine in the middle of the river (Peet, 1877).

Those who could escape did so within minutes. Passengers trapped in the wreckage soon faced a horrible confrontation with flames erupting from the train's heating stoves.

The Fire and the Orders Not to Put it Out

In 1876, passenger cars, like those linked in the Pacific Express, were made of highly varnished wood and heated with wood-burning stoves. Ohio Law required that heating stoves be equipped to self-extinguish, if the railcar was subjected to severe mechanical shock or vibration. Unfortunately, the LS&MS Railway, like many other railroad companies of that time, used conventional stoves due to cost and the doubt that a stove could be designed to self-extinguish. With much of the Pacific Express reduced to splinters of dry, varnished wood, and with well-stoked fires in stoves suddenly turned topsy-turvy, fire arose from both ends of the wreck. Before the fire raged out of control, at least four men were quickly on the scene to render aid: Henry Apthorp, superintendent of telegraph repairs for Western Union and the LS&MS; Michael Tinley, saloon keeper at one of the hotels; James Manning, foreman of the fire engine Lake Erie; Charles Philbrook, LS&MS head painter in Ashtabula.

Clearly, the pump engine closest to the wreck was ready for use, and the fire hose of the Lake Erie, usable with the pump engine, was only six hundred yards away. Based on eyewitness accounts, the entire wreck was ablaze within seven to ten minutes after the fall of the last car. Screams came from the wreckage as the blaze intensified. The Ashtabula Volunteer Fire Department arrived at the site with their hand fire engine Protection and the steamer fire engine Neptune. Although its firehouse alarm bell was sounded shortly after the Pacific Express fell, the hand-fire-engine Lake Erie never left its quarters near the train station and the wreck.

Mr. Strong, station agent for the LS&MS Ashtabula Station, arrived after the firemen and relieved Henry Apthorp of command of the scene. Strong asked Apthorp what was to be done. Apthorp replied, "Get men to help up the wounded" (Peet, 1877). G. W. Knapp, the Ashtabula fire chief, arrived on the scene afterward, and asked Strong where the water should be thrown. Strong's reply was that water not be put on the fire and to aid the wounded. Firemen began to lay hose and were told by an official of the LS&MS that water would be of no use. Fire Chief Knapp, known to be slow in taking initiative, followed instructions of railroad officials and did not give any orders to attack the fire. On their own, the firefighters procured buckets from the general store and established a bucket brigade in a vain attempt to put down the fire. This action did allow for the rescue of Columbia fireman Peter Livenbroe, who died later as a result of his injuries en route to the hospital in Cleveland. Eventually, firemen and equipment returned to quarters, leaving the wreck ablaze.

Testimony later given to the Coroner's Jury indicated concern for the fire engines freezing, and that was the reason for the order to return to quarters. After three-and-a-half hours of burning, most wood in the train would have been consumed, leaving firemen to believe the fire would burn itself out within an hour-or-so. Modern forensic science has identified a "wicking effect," in which a very hot fire (1000 degrees Fahrenheit) slowly burns (twelve to eighteen hours), and the victim's own clothing acts as a candlewick. If bodies of passengers were burned in this manner, only ankles and feet would remain, since there is not enough fatty tissue and related oils in the feet and ankles to sustain or fuel the "wick." That is the reason baskets of shoes would be found in the days following, some with feet still in the shoes.

For that same reason, by 6:00 a.m. the next day, December 30, the wreck was still smoldering. Railroad officials had likely followed a general practice of the day to let train wrecks burn. The practice may have been traced to the inability to extinguish such fires, although it might also have suited the railroads, which did not have to pay out as much in liabilities if persons could not be proven to have been on board the wrecked train.

Given the facts of the fire as they are known today, it can be said with certainty that the Ashtabula Volunteer Fire Department was not prepared for an incident of such magnitude. (A similar wreck, involving a single LS&MS passenger coach had occurred nine years earlier at Angola, New York, "The Angola Horror," too distant to be particularly instructive to Ashtabula firemen.) Realizing that trapped survivors were allowed to burn to death even after arrival of the fire department, Fire Chief Knapp, Station Agent Strong, and Superintendent Apthorp should have been formally charged, as a result of not issuing orders to attack the flames. Also, it was the duty of Michael Tinley, foreman of the fire engine Lake Erie, to have placed his engine into service with the aid of bystanders at the station platform. Hose from the Lake Erie could have been brought to the scene prior to the fire's raging out of control, and connected to the station pump engine, or it could have drawn water from the river. Such action would likely have saved at least some of those who perished. Tinley, as ranking member of the fire department initially on the site, should have taken command of the rescue effort until relieved by the fire chief himself. Tinley, then, was solely responsible for allowing the fire to get out of control, if we narrow the Coroner's Jury finding of responsibility resting on "those first to arrive" at the scene. No indictments were ever made. However, by 1878, Tinley, Knapp and other senior fire department officials had been relieved of their leadership roles, as a result of their action in the incident.

The Next Morning and the Aftermath

At midnight, the wreck scene was abandoned, except for an expressman guarding valuables in the onboard safes. The wreck scene at midnight was described as both appalling and terrifying. The dead littered the area, with many burned beyond recognition. Some bodies were recovered from the wreckage but left lying on the ground in the snow, after the chaos of those few hours. At 1:15 a.m., a train arrived from Cleveland with the LS&MS superintendent, the assistant superintendent, the train dispatcher, and five surgeons from the Homeopathic College. The surgeons were sent immediately to injured crewmen, specifically to engineer Folsom and fireman Livenbroe of the locomotive Columbia. Ashtabula surgeons had already attended to wounded passengers in homes, and in makeshift circumstances in hotels and saloons, there being no hospital in Ashtabula at the time. Twenty of the wounded, including Folsom and Livenbroe, were taken by train to the hospital in Cleveland. The remainder of the injured were left in the care of Ashtabula physicians. First light, on the morning of December 30, gave a true look at the scope of the night's carnage. The sight was charred ruins, bent frames of passenger cars, wheels, bridge iron, and the locomotive Columbia. Even more horrible than the wreckage, burned bodies and body parts were strewn throughout the scene. Firefighter Fred Blakeslee, a photographer by occupation, was on the scene early in the morning, taking photographs so that an official record could be kept. The LS&MS immediately sent workers down to recover bodies and relics from the wreckage. In many cases, personal effects recovered were the only clues to identifying passengers suspected of being on the train.

Many personal effects and valuables thought to have been stolen from the injured and dead were recovered by the intervention of Ashtabula Mayor H. P. Hepburn. LS&MS Chief Engineer Charles Collins wept like a baby at the first sight of the wreck site, and he personally assisted in the search for bodies. Over the next several days, friends and families arrived in Ashtabula in waves, in hopes of finding some trace of a loved one. One such search was the one for Miss Minnie Mixer, of Buffalo, described as a beautiful young woman, recently graduated from a private school. Active in her church and choir, she had been bridesmaid in the wedding of her closest friend only the week prior. In the City of Buffalo, she looked forward to joining friends to celebrate the New Year. After the crash, her parents came to Ashtabula to search but found not a trace of her or her belongings. After her father had all but given up, her mother found among the disaster site's harvested effects a chain that was her daughter's.

News media telegraphed the story of the wreck coast-to-coast and began referring to the tragedy as the "Ashtabula Horror." The media sensationalized the disaster with stories of horror, such as those published in *Harper's Weekly*. The wreckage of the bridge was gradually removed to the LS&MS yards in Cleveland. On January 18, 1877, just twenty days after the accident, a wooden Howe truss replacement bridge was put in place, and rail traffic was restored.

Over the years since the disaster, several bridges were installed at the site, until finally, a set of twin concrete portals was completed in 1904, effectively creating twin culverts through which the Ashtabula River passes, while supporting trains crossing the gulf.

Ashtabula Coroner's Jury

Wasting no time, a jury assembled Saturday, December 30, the day following the accident. Ashtabula citizens chosen for service included: H. L. Morrison, T. D. Faulkner, Edward G. Pierce, George W. Dickinson, Henry H. Perry, and F. A. Pettibone. Edward W. Richards, justice of the peace, was the acting coroner, and Theodore Hall was chosen as the jury's counsel. The investigation lasted sixty-eight days, in search of relevant facts and the causes of the tragedy. Jury members felt it their duty, rather than simply to say victims died as a result of the bridge failing, to determine if the bridge failed due to its plan and design, its construction, or it maintenance, and to determine how the fire might have been extinguished. Was inaction on the fire due to stupidity, selfish carelessness, or malevolent intent? The jury wanted to reach accurate findings and ultimately to prevent such a disaster from ever reoccurring.

In addition to citizens, railroad officials, the mayor, fire officials, and passengers, the Coroner's Jury heard from engineers and bridge builders: Albert H. Howland, C. E.; Job Abbott, C. E. and vice president of the Canton Bridge Company of Canton, Ohio; A. Gottleib, C. E. and superintendent of the Western Department of the Keystone Bridge Company, headquartered in Chicago; E. N. Beebout, C. E.; Joseph Tomlinson, who drew the plans for the bridge under direction of Amasa Stone (*Ashtabula News Extra*, 1877). The professional engineers generally agreed in their disapproval of the Howe Truss Plan for wrought-iron bridges over long spans, and in affirming that, the top chord (bridge deck) and main braces were deficient. They also disapproved the lack of physical connection between the main braces and angle blocks in the top chord, which appear, ultimately, to be the single element most responsible for the bridge's collapse.

Findings of the Coroner's Jury were: (1)That at about 7:30 p.m., Friday, December 29, 1876, the iron bridge of the LS&MS Railway gave way, leaving a sixty-foot chasm into which the train was precipitated. (2)In their fall, the railcars were partially destroyed by crushing, and their destruction was completed by a conflagration immediately following, kindled by fire from the stoves. (3)That the fall of the bridge was the result of defects and errors made in designing, constructing, and erecting it; that a great defect, and one which appears in many parts of the structure, was the dependence of every member for its efficient action upon the probability that all or nearly all other members would retain their position and do the duty for which they were designed, instead of giving to each member a positive connection with the rest, which nothing but a direct rupture could sever. The members of each truss were, instead of being fastened together, rested one upon the other, for example: the deficient cross-section of portions of the top chords and some of the main braces, and insufficient lugs or flanges to keep the ends of the main and counterbraces from slipping out of place; the construction of the packing and yokes used in binding together the main and counterbraces at the points where they crossed each other; the shimming of the top chords to compensate deficient length of some of their members; the placing, during the process of erection, of thick beams where the plan required thin ones, and thin ones where it required thick ones. (4)The railway company used and continued to use the bridge for about eleven years, during which time a careful inspection by a competent bridge engineer could not have failed to discover all these defects. For the neglect of such careful inspection, the railway company alone was responsible. (5)The responsibility of the disaster and its consequent loss of life rests upon the railway company, which, by its chief executive officer, planned and erected the bridge. (6)The cars in which deceased passengers were carried into the chasm were not heated by heating apparatuses constructed so that the fire would be immediately extinguished when the cars were thrown from the track or overturned. The railroad's failure to comply with the provisions of the law places the responsibility of the origin of the fire upon them. (7)The responsibility for not putting out the fire at the time it first made its appearance in the wreck rests upon those who were first to arrive at the scene of the disaster, and who seemed to have been so overwhelmed by the fearful calamity that they lost all presence of mind and failed to use the means at hand, including the steam pump in the pumping house and the fire engine Lake Erie and its hose, which might have been attached to the steam pump in time to save lives. The steamer belonging to the fire department and also the Protection fire engine were hauled more than a mile through a blinding snowstorm and over roads rendered almost impassable by drifted snow, and arrived on the ground too late to save human life. But nothing should have prevented the chief fireman from making all possible efforts to extinguish what fire then remained. For his failure to do this, he is responsible. (8)The deceased persons, whose bodies were identified and whose bodies and parts of bodies were unidentified, came to their deaths by the precipitation of the railcars, in which they were riding, into the valley of Ashtabula Creek due to the falling of the bridge, and the crushing and burning of the railcars; for all of which the railway company is responsible.

Ohio Legislature
January 12, 1877, the Legislature of Ohio passed a resolution "that a joint committee be appointed to investigate the cause or causes of the recent accident." The Joint Committee and civil engineers Benjamin F. Bowen, Thomas H. Johnson, and John Graham reported to the Legislature January 30, 1877 (Gasparini and Fields, 1993). The engineers made the following criticisms of the design. (1)The Howe truss could be made safe for a 150-foot iron span but would be excessively heavy. (2)The compressive diagonal braces were intermixed with different

sizes, creating unique stress levels in each brace of the same diagonal. (3)The end bearings due to design modifications were not square and tended to be rounded. (4)There were no positive physical connections between the braces and angle blocks to prevent movement. (5)The compressive elements in the top chord of the bridge were intermixed with different sized I-beams that were not continuously tied together. (6)The chord was placed in flexure by trainloads and was laterally braced at every other panel point. (7)The vertical "X" bracing between trusses and between the top and bottom chords of the bridge were determined to be inadequate. (8)The vertical lugs on the angle blocks would have been stronger, had they been continuous. (9)The engineers reported that failure of the Ashtabula bridge occurred in the second and third panels of the south truss, counting from the west abutment. They did not estimate the snowload and considered the load from the wind to be negligible, even though it was reported as being twenty-four to fifty-four miles per hour. The conclusions of the engineers were: "The failure was not due to any defective quality in the iron. It was not owing to the sudden effect of intense cold, for failure occurred by bending, and not by breaking. It was not the result of a weakness gradually developed after the erection of the bridge. It was due simply to the fact that it was not constructed in accordance with certain well-established engineering principles" (Gasparini and Fields, 1993).

Amasa Stone testified before the Joint Committee and adamantly denied any wrongdoing, stating that the bridge design was sound. Stone's explanation of the collapse was that the train derailed upon the bridge and caused it to fail. Another reason he gave was that the snowstorm that hit Ashtabula created a tornado that smashed the bridge as the Pacific Express crossed. Engineer Albert H. Howland, likely on behalf of the Coroner's Jury in Ashtabula, reported to the Joint Committee February 12, 1877, concluding that failure occurred at the second set of vertical rods counting from west to east. He believed failure likely resulted from the buckling outward of the three I-beams that were continuous at that point (Gasparini and Fields, 1993).

The Joint Committee drafted provisions for a bill to be brought before the Ohio Legislature. The provisions included a bridge design code, required bridge specifications and expert review of designs, construction supervision, and periodic inspection by engineers. The proposed expert reviewer was to be an individual who passed an examination given by a panel of at least three members of the American Society of Civil Engineers (Gasparini and Fields, 1993). The Ohio Legislature, likely as a result of Amasa Stone's and the railroads' collective influence, never made the provisions into law.

Curiously, Chief Engineer Charles Collins was found dead from a gunshot wound to the head from an apparent suicide, just days after testimony before the Joint Committee. A subsequent autopsy reported, however, that given the angle of the points of entry, the wounds were inconsistent with suicide. (See Appendices B and C.) This left murder as the only possibility, but the autopsy report was quietly buried only to be discovered nearly a century later. Later, Amasa Stone also committed suicide, May 10, 1883, likely because of public opinion blaming him for the Ashtabula bridge disaster. Tyler Dennett, a biographer, wrote that Stone had "lived over into a technological age which he did not understand and for which a carpenter's rule of thumb was not sufficient."

The American Society of Civil Engineers

Charles MacDonald conducted a third investigation of the bridge failure for the American Society of Civil Engineers (ASCE). He reported his findings to the ASCE on February 21,1877. MacDonald agreed with other engineers regarding calculations of static and live loads on the bridge. He also reported in candid fashion that the breaking resistance limits of the diagonal I-beams were 13,300 pounds per square inch as designed, and as low as 4,433 pounds per square inch, assuming the beam ends to be completely rounded (as described in some testimonies). MacDonald stated that there was nothing to use as a guide to determine where the actual breaking resistance lay between these limits. He went further in stating that the value of 4,433 pounds per square inch value was so low that the bridge would never have stood on its own. He concluded that the breaking resistance was generally adequate given that the bridge had been in continuous service for eleven years prior to the disaster (Gasparini and Fields, 1993). MacDonald was the only investigating engineer to have discovered a flaw with the bridge's superstructure. In his report, MacDonald stated: "The cast iron angle block at the top of the second set of braces had the south lug broken off close to the face, and the line of fracture disclosed an air hole extending over one half the entire section." Based on this evidence, he reported his conclusion " failure first began in the south truss, at the second panel point from the west abutment at the second top chord angle block, whose south lug was impaired by an air hole as to be reduced in strength fully one half" (Gasparini and Fields, 1993). MacDonald showed that, after repeated load cycles over the course of eleven years of service, the south lug was subjected to severe fatigue stress. The cold (sixteen degrees Fahrenheit) of December 29, 1876, caused the fracture strength of the cast iron on the south lug to be considerably reduced. Given these two facts, MacDonald's conclusion as reported was that the load force generated by the locomotives, Socrates and Columbia, caused the south lug of the second angle block to become unstable and shear off. Given the lack of positive mechanical connections in the Ashtabula bridge's superstructure, the broken lug caused the I-beams supporting the bridge deck to bow outward in a southernly direction and to sink slightly, until the compressive diagonal beams slipped away from the underside of the second angle block, thereby setting up a cascade failure of the remaining angle blocks and support beams in the bridge's superstructure.

MacDonald recommended the inspection of bridges by professionals only and called for studies on the behavior of compressive elements in bridges. By 1888, bridge standards for design forbade the use of cast iron on any part of a bridge structure.

Consequences of the Bridge Design

In the years to follow, no bridges of steel or iron were built of a design in which the components of said bridge acted in an independent manner to maintain structural integrity. All components were designed and built to act as one by providing a positive connection between the braces, counterbraces, and other bridge components to provide the intended strength and durability necessary in a railroad environment. Also by 1888, the use of cast iron in the bridge design superstructure was forbidden. The LS&MS, by the early 1900s, eliminated a majority of the long bridges on its main line similar to the one in Ashtabula with fill and large culverts (some thirty to forty feet in height) as part of its four-track main line project. The death of rail baron "Commodore" Cornelius Vanderbilt occurred in January 1877. Vanderbilt, who had been in poor health for many years, was controlling shareholder of the New York Central and Hudson River Railroad and the LS&MS Railway. While no one knows for certain, his death may have been hastened by the horror and suddenness of the tragedy in Ashtabula. Government regulation, in the years that followed, created the Interstate Commerce Commission (ICC) whose original purpose was to regulate safety and investigate accidents of the American railroad companies. The ICC in time gave way to the U. S. Department of Transportation's Federal Railroad Administration as the governing body of railway safety.

At the time of the disaster, Ashtabula, Cleveland, and Lorain were the prominent cities in northern Ohio and were approximately equivalent in population and physical size. As a result of this disaster, growth in the city of Ashtabula was almost brought to a halt, and significant growth was delayed until the early twentieth century. Cleveland and Lorain, in the late nineteenth century, grew into large cities, while Ashtabula remained in a semi-state of stagnation. The lack of growth may result from Ashtabula's becoming synonymous with the worst rail disaster in history. Growth in Ashtabula Harbor continued throughout the late nineteenth century under the development of the LS&MS Railway and Ashtabula, Youngstown, and Pittsburgh Railroad.

Memorial Monument
To commemorate the twentieth anniversary of the accident, the citizens of Ashtabula and the LS&MS Railway Company erected a granite monument in Chestnut Grove Cemetery in memory of "the unrecognized dead." As a result of the accident, the need for a hospital became apparent, and Ashtabula citizens built the city's first hospital at a site a quarter mile north of the bridge. This site was chosen as it was central to the LS&MS's Ashtabula Railroad Yards and station, the Ashtabula, Youngstown, and Pittsburgh's Ashtabula Railroad Yards, and the docks served by both railroads in Ashtabula Harbor.

Approximately ten years after the disaster, the LS&MS Railway Company adopted the use of steam heat in all passenger cars, replacing the dangerous wood/coal stoves responsible for the fires at Ashtabula and other notable nineteenth century railroad accidents. Today, passenger cars are heated with electrical heating appliances.

Works Consulted

Gasparini, D. A. and Melissa Fields. "Collapse of Ashtabula Bridge on December 29, 1876," *Journal of Performance of Constructed Facilities,* 1993.

Peet, Stephen D. *The Ashtabula Disaster.* Chicago, 1877.

Reed, Robert C. *Train Wrecks.* New York, 1968.

Shaw, Robert B. *Down Brakes.* London, 1961.

Whittle, Daniel W. *Memoirs of Philip P. Bliss.* New York, 1877.

Williams Brothers. *History of Ashtabula County,* Philadelphia, 1878.

P. P. Bliss and Late Nineteenth-Century Urban Revivalism
Timothy M. Kalil

Timothy Kalil grew up in Ashtabula hearing the history and lore of the bridge disaster from his family. He became more familiar with the disaster through playing and singing the hymns written by P. P. Bliss, who was a passenger on the train.

Gospel hymn composer P. P. Bliss died in 1876 along with other passengers, including his wife, Lucy, in the "Great Ashtabula (Ohio) Train Disaster," sometimes called "The Ashtabula Bridge Disaster," December 29, 1876. He was en route from his home in Rome, Pennsylvania, to assist evangelist Dwight L. Moody in Chicago when the accident occurred.[1] His two children, Philip Paul (1872–1933) and George Goodwin (1874–1933), remained at home in Rome, Pennsylvania. In a brief span of time, Bliss lived a fruitful and creative life.

Bliss was part of the late-nineteenth century phenomenon of "urban revivalism" in America—a movement that focused on mass Christian conversions and saving souls in urban areas/cities where crowds could more easily assemble. Cities included a diversity of people, the poor, immigrants (seventeen million Europeans between 1892 and 1924), and persons with no religious involvement, or a lapsed religious experience—"the unsaved."[2] Most cities had large-capacity venues, such as music halls, theaters and auditoriums. Chicago, then considered "the

---

1 Bobby Joe Neil, "Philip P. Bliss (1838–1876): Gospel Hymn Composer and Compiler" (Unpublished dissertation, New Orleans Baptist Theological Seminary, 1977) pp. 33–42.

2 www.ellisisland.org

Midwest City," was as an ideal location for mass evangelism, as it was a railroad and lakeport hub.

Although Bliss's musical education was "erratic," it was typical of many mid-nineteenth century musicians. He briefly attended singing schools and music conventions. In addition, he attended the Normal Academy of Music in Geneseo, New York (1860, 1861, and 1863) and received important private instruction.

Despite his limited background, Bliss began his professional music career as a teacher of music in 1859. Between 1859 and 1865, Bliss was befriended and influenced by the composer and publisher George F. Root, who became somewhat of a mentor to Bliss, as the two corresponded frequently. Perhaps, as a result, Bliss, like Root, integrated secular musical elements into his gospel hymns.

From about 1840 to 1870, a primary venue for musically attracting large numbers of people with religious purposes in mind was the Sunday school, and concurrently and later, the "great prayer meetings," and "services of praise." Many early religious composers, including Bliss, first came into music evangelism as teachers of singing schools and/or through Sunday schools.

Bliss arrived in Chicago in 1865 to assist the music firm of Root & Cady by singing in a vocal quartet, "Yankee Boys." Although the quartet idea was never fully realized, the firm asked Bliss to stay as a promoter of its music publications through schools and conventions.

Several propitious events had an impact on Bliss's professional life. In 1869, he met evangelist Dwight L. Moody who eventually convinced him in 1874 to become a music evangelist. In 1870, he met evangelist Major Daniel W. Whittle, who recommended him for a position as choir director of the First Congregational Church of Chicago, and a short while later he became superintendent of the Sunday school there. Bliss left his church position in 1874 and dedicated himself to full-time music evangelism, traveling with evangelist Whittle to gospel meetings in the Midwest and the South.

Bliss's first published song was "Lora Vale" in 1864. It was composed in the sentimental style of the parlor song as, for example, Stephen Foster's "Beautiful Dreamer," so popular in the midcentury years. Having began his music career with a secular song, by the end of his life, Bliss had written approximately ninety-five secular songs and three hundred sacred songs. He occasionally used a nom de plume for secular songs, "Pro Phundo Basso" (in Italian opera, profundo basso meaning "profound bass"), standing for his initials, "P. P. B." The alternative name demonstrated his sense of humor.

After the Civil War, Bliss and other composers' Sunday school hymns increasingly were infused with the popular melodies and rhythms of the day and with conventional harmonies, elegant and descriptive words, sentimentality, and dotted rhythms. *The Triumph* and *The Prize,* collections of Sunday school songs assembled by Bliss, both published by Root & Cady in 1870, exhibited a new trend, ushering in the "gospel hymn era" beginning about 1870. As such, Bliss's gospel hymns show secular influences from Italian opera, Irish and Scottish melodies, minstrelsy, "barbershop quartet" harmonies, and marches. In addition, composers such as Bliss provided a variety of moods and styles in their gospel hymns—from the stately to the rollicking. The mass appeal of the "new" gospel hymns, then, accommodated the mass audiences of the emerging urban revival movement.[3]

Moody discovered that music evangelists and the new hymns/hymnals that they produced spoke to the masses, complemented his sermons, and increased interest and the number of souls being saved. Thus developed in the 1870s, the classic evangelistic preaching and music teams of "Moody and

---

3 P. P. Bliss, *Gospel Songs, A Choice Collection of Hymns and Tunes, New and Old* (Cincinnati, 1874) and *P. P. Bliss and Ira Sankey, Gospel Hymns and Sacred Songs* (Chicago and Cincinnati, 1875); reprint (selected songs), Thomas E. Corts, ed., *Songs of Bliss* (Birmingham, AL, 2002).

Sankey," "Whittle and Bliss," and later, "Billy Sunday and Homer Rodeheaver," even today's Billy Graham and George Beverly Shea. Moody and Sankey's formula was stated as: "Mr. Moody will preach the gospel; Mr. Sankey will sing the gospel." Some other late-nineteenth century hymn authors and/or composers include: Root, James McGranahan, Sankey, W. H. Doane, George C. Stebbins, Robert Lowry, H. R. Palmer, Philip Phillips, and the blind poet, Fanny J. Crosby.

Three collections by Bliss use the names "gospel hymn" or "gospel song" for the first time in the context of late-nineteenth urban revivalism. John Church and Company of Cincinnati published the first, entitled *Gospel Songs* (1874). Stated Bliss: "I am preparing a book of gospel songs for our special use. . . . All good in it must come from God."[4]

About 1873, Sankey prepared a musical "scrapbook" for his planned trip to the British Isles. It consisted mostly of gospel songs by Bliss and others. The songs in the scrapbook became the basis for an inexpensive printed songbook in 1873, *Sacred Songs and Solos*. Sankey affirms: "This collection contained a number of Mr. Bliss's best songs, which together with a companion book of 'Words Only' (the latter being sold for a penny) is believed to have attained a larger circulation than any collection of hymns and tunes ever published."[5]

Upon his return from a successful tour of the British Isles, Sankey approached Bliss about combining their hymnals into a joint publication. The result was *Gospel Hymns and Sacred Songs* (1875), followed by *Gospel Hymns No. 2* (1876), published by John Church and Company and Bigelow and Main. The latter hymnal culminated in six editions published as *Gospel Hymns Nos. 1–6*, completed (739 hymns) in 1894 that became a staple in the world of gospel hymnody.

Declared William J. Reynolds: "The main stream of gospel

---

4 Daniel W. Whittle, ed., *Memoirs of Philip P. Bliss* (New York, 1877) p. 243; Bliss quoted in Neil, "Philip P. Bliss," p. 140.

5 Ibid, Sankey quoted in Neil, "Philip P. Bliss," p. 147.

hymnody followed *Gospel Hymns,* and this series remained unchallenged to the end of the century. Gospel songs, which first appeared in other collections, later became immensly [sic] popular through their inclusion in one of these six editions." [6]

The classic gospel hymn as developed by Bliss and others features verse-chorus (two-part) form, major keys, four-part harmonies, with the melody in the top voice, and various textual devices including "echo voices" (imitative voices) and bass "lead ins" (two or three notes sung solo). Preferred meters are 3/4, 4/4, and 6/8 (respectively, 3, 4, and 6 beats per measure), while rhythms are "catchy." An example (though not a gospel song) is the use of dotted/march rhythms as in "The Battle Hymn of the Republic." [7]

Although Bliss used the melodeon in mass meetings, in general, the piano is the preferred instrument. In addition, most melodies are within range for amateur singers, and the piano accompaniment is within the capacity of the average pianist. These factors made the music appealing to common persons. Many of the basic musical characteristics are seen in Bliss's "The Light of the World" (Is Jesus), "Let the Lower Lights Be Burning," and "Jesus Loves Even Me." In addition, Horatio G. Spafford and Bliss's "It Is Well" (with My Soul) is also instructive for the "echo effect" between voices. [8]

Texts are strophic (upon repeat of the music a different verse is used). In regards to the textual content, Eskew and Downey state:

> Gospel hymns are generally subjective or hortatory, are often addressed to one's fellow man, and center upon a single theme which emphasized through repetitions of individual phrases and refrain following each stanza. The poems deal with such subjects as conversion, atonement through Christ,

6 Neil, "Philip P. Bliss," p. 159.

7 Harry Eskew and James C. Downey, "Gospel Music," in *The New Grove Dictionary of American Music,* 1986.

8 Bliss, *Gospel Songs,* pp. 80, 63, 55, and 42.

the assurance of salvation, and the joys of heaven; their character ranges from the militant and didactic to the meditative and devotional. The music is generally composed for a specific text. [9]

In accordance with the genre's mass appeal, the text of a gospel hymn also usually features an abundance of metaphors. As such, these metaphors provided "visual" magnification of the words and music that aided the appeal. For example, in Bliss's "Hold the Fort!," "good versus evil," etc., is told in mostly military terms. "Comrades" (believers) are asked to have "courage" and to "hold the fort" (keep the faith) and fight the "battle" against the "foe" (Satan) until reinforcements and their "Commander" (Jesus) "appears" to lead them to "victory" and "triumph." This song, written in 1870, was based on a true, heroic Civil War story related to Bliss by Major Whittle. The expression "hold the fort" in current American parlance derives from the title of this popular gospel hymn.[10]

Bliss helped to codify and name the genre known as the "gospel hymn" or "gospel song" through his publications, music evangelism, compositional and textual style, and charisma. He and Ira Sankey, as part of an interdenominational emphasis, made music and interdenominationalism an inextricable part of urban revivalism/evangelism. Twenty Bliss hymns are in use today, worldwide. Bliss's late career refusal of royalty payments and his donation to charitable causes, and his "martyr-like" death are considered models of Christian behavior. He integrated secular musical elements into his hymns and set the stage for such later composers as Thomas A. Dorsey, "The Father of Black Gospel Music" who added blues and jazz elements to the hymn, creating a new improvisational genre about 1930.[11]

---

9 Op. cit.

10 Bliss, *Gospel Songs,* p. 25.

11 Timothy M. Kalil, "The Role of the Great Migration of African-Americans to Chicago in the Development of Traditional Black Gospel Piano by Thomas A. Dorsey, Circa 1930" (Ph.D. diss., Kent State University, 1993) pp. 115–172.

Selected Bibliography

Bliss, P. P. *Gospel Songs, A Choice Collection of Hymns and Tunes, New and Old.* Cincinnati: John Church and Company, 1874.

Bliss, P. P. and Ira Sankey. *Gospel Hymns and Sacred Songs.* Chicago: Bigelow and Main, and Cincinnati: John Church and Company, 1875.

Corts, Thomas E. ed. *Songs of Bliss.* Birmingham, AL: Samford University Press, 2002.

Eskew, Harry and James C. Downey. "Gospel Music," in *The New Grove Dictionary of American Music,* 1986.

Gasparini, D. A. and Melissa Fields. "Collapse of Ashtabula Bridge on December 29, 1876," *Journal of Performance of Constructed Facilities,* 1993.

Kalil, Timothy M. "The Role of the Great Migration of African-Americans to Chicago in the Development of Traditional Black Gospel Piano by Thomas A. Dorsey, Circa 1930." Unpublished Ph.D. dissertation Kent State University, 1993.

Neil, Bobby Joe. "Philip P. Bliss (1838–1876): Gospel Hymn Composer and Compiler." Unpublished dissertation, New Orleans Baptist Theological Seminary, 1977.

Peet, Stephen D. *The Ashtabula Disaster.* Chicago, 1877.

Reed, Robert C. *Train Wrecks.* New York, 1968.

Shaw, Robert B. *Down Brakes.* London, 1961.

Whittle, Daniel W. ed. *Memoirs of Philip P. Bliss.* New York, 1877.

Williams Brothers. *History of Ashtabula County.* Philadelphia, 1878.

In Search of the Story
David G. Tobias

"He's that crazy man who digs holes in the gulf." That's how David Tobias is known around Ashtabula, a title he cherishes. By his own admission, he is a tinkerer, who loves history and finding historical artifacts. He was raised in Ashtabula, and therefore, has had many opportunities to carefully gather and preserve objects from the site, some of which are pictured in this volume.

Man proposes: God disposes. And when all is done, man returns to pick up the pieces of his history, to try to make some sense of it. And yet, these pieces, little fragments of time, of destiny, of love and hope and loss—what use shall we make of them? Are they to be left undisturbed to deteriorate? Should they be gathered into shelves of a storage room or museum? Might they become idols of devotion? Perhaps these residual elements of great events are left to remind us of the brevity of life, of the fact that our most cherished possessions could someday be mere artifacts and curiosities.

Perhaps, with an event such as the Ashtabula bridge disaster, the leftover "relics" from the lives of others make us conscious of heroes and godly men and women who helped others at great personal risk, and who were injured or even lost their lives in the effort to assist others. We recognize P. P. Bliss for his remarkable musical achievements and his devotion to our Lord Jesus Christ. But maybe the reminders of those people and their experiences serve to show us how we should act under pressure, and to show us how temporary things on earth really are.

A hundred years from now, it will not matter how much money you had, the sort of house you lived in, or the kind of car you drove. But the world may be different because you were important in the life of a child, to someone in need, or some disaster victim.

It has been more than 125 years, and people are still talking about the Ashtabula bridge disaster of December 29, 1876. It is as compelling to local folks as Custer's Battle Site, or Civil War venues, or natural splendor like Niagara Falls. To stand on the very spot where something of significance occurred is forever to feel a part of that event. People have documented good and bad responses to the Ashtabula accident, decisions that shaped individuals. Character was made, and character was lost that day, December 29, 1876. Ashtabula's citizens said at the time: (1)"This night and its events will have an effect for a long time to come." (2)"The accident has been bad enough." (3)"It is like we are under a shadow, a dark cloud."

Anyone who has ever read Peet's book, *The Ashtabula Disaster,* or who reads this book, will likely never again pass the site so casually, or never again consider that fateful night as just a historical fact. It is a touching, compelling, moving story that makes you a part of something bigger. It makes you care. It changes your heart.

Many questions linger on the historical horizon. Why did such a tragedy have to happen here in the little, unprepared, ill-equipped community of Ashtabula? Why did Ashtabula's leaders not respond more decisively to put out the fire, to rescue the injured? Why did citizens not rise up against the brazenness of evil men, robbing corpses and taking advantage of the terribly injured? What drives us to keep exploring, looking for answers even 125 years after the disaster? Perhaps erection of the monument in 1895, almost twenty years after the tragedy, was actually an attempt to find closure. Maybe even such attempts as the 2002 symposium and this very volume represent a quest for closure. The dead have been buried, the wreckage hauled away, the bridge replaced, and monuments have been erected. Still, we wonder.

We occasionally find what we do not seek, but more often it

is the sought that is found. The Ashtabula bridge disaster attracts historians, writers, railroad fans, architects and engineers, religious people, Christian teachers, archeologists, and treasure-hunters. Most find at least some of what they are seeking. I have certainly found some interesting artifacts.

The newspapers of that day suggested that the Ashtabula railroad-bridge disaster had almost all the elements of the perfect horror, in that it included the dark night, the heavy snowfall, a fierce wind, bitter cold, the modern technology of the railway, height, a bridge, fire, water, and an inaccessible site. The disaster is a story, and for those of us who live here or once lived here, it is our story. I like to hear about something, research it, find it, map it, study it, touch it, preserve it, and feel it—both physically and emotionally. Thoreau once said, "I wanted to know the cold by feeling it in my hands and body, not by reading about it in a book."

Someone once said that "the past is a bucket of ashes." Well, I am the type that likes to collect those buckets of ashes, and sift through them to see what man has left behind. For a person such as I, truly great sites from which to sift such buckets are very hard to find, difficult to leave, and impossible to forget. A writer once said, "The past is not the property of historians; it is public possession. It belongs to anyone who is aware of it, and it grows by being shared." (William Havighurst).

A disaster is a time capsule. Everything is sealed in a very short passing of time, whether it burns, freezes, sinks, falls, gets buried, or is simply left and forgotten. Every piece from a disaster site tells a story, and I like stories.

To this day, the site of the Ashtabula bridge disaster is impressive. Two large arches span the gulf and frame a still somewhat wild and hard-to-reach area. The train whistles still blow. Trains still pass overhead. Fishermen still vie for the best spots along the river. To get there, one drives to Cedarquist Park. Simply follow the river downstream via trails. The deer, fox, turkeys, squirrels, ducks, geese, and other wildlife will likely be there to greet you, as they have been for decades. Somehow, they add their own natural charm to a place that suffered the horror of that December night more than a century ago.

My first experience was simply site work. I walked down the gulf, looked at the ground, and saw part of well walls exposed, the foundations of the pump house where the first victims were taken, and picked up brass screws, melted brass, railroad spikes, coupling pins, nuts and bolts, and an occasional coin. I used the same recovery methods they used 125 years ago, digging and scraping with rakes and shovels. With the arrival of quality metal detection instruments, a whole new world was opened. But what became obvious was that the site was literally one solid mass of melted metal. You could hardly tune a metal detector down there because of so much metal.

Since the area has seen five or more bridges, with replacements, etc., it was difficult to know what object belonged to which bridge or which era. However, to me, everything was of value. I cleaned it, preserved it, and sought to understand it. Over the years, some items found include: a melted one dollar U.S. gold piece; a pre-1876 love token; shield nickels; a pre-1876 Canadian quarter (actually, my daughter found it, though a fisherman's boot print was right beside it); bullets; a knife; silver and gold jewelry; melted brass fixtures. Melted gold, silver, lead, and glass demonstrate just how hot it had to have been in that fire in 1876. Lead melts at about 621 degrees; silver at 1,800 degrees; gold at 1,950 degrees; brass and copper at about 1,981–2,000 degrees. Everything I have found speaks of a horrible cold night, yet how hot it became.

The river flows heavy at times, rising to flood stage with the Spring thaws, though it almost completely dries up in the summer. How much evidence has been washed away so casually in the rise and fall of the water flow? How much might be interred undisturbed far down the river bed? It all adds to the charm and mystery of that unusual event.

The Pacific Express, Train No. 5 and the Wreckage

1. Socrates, the lead engine, was a 32-ton locomotive with Dan McGuire as the engineer and James Hunt as fireman. Both McGuire and Hunt survived, due to McGuire's quick thinking, pulling the throttle as he began to sense a sudden uphill ascent, just as the bridge was giving way.

2. Columbia, the second locomotive or "booster" engine, 35 tons, fell to the bottom of the gulf with its clock stopped at 7:32 p.m. The engineer was Gustavus "Pap" Folsom, and the fireman was Peter Livenbroe. Both survived the fall, but Livenbroe died January 3 in a Cleveland hospital. Folsom had been going 12–15 miles-per-hour, but was applying the air brake on Columbia, just as McGuire was unexpectedly opening the throttle on Socrates. The two engines uncoupled, the Socrates and its tender making it safely onto the abutment, and Columbia striking the abutment on the way down.

3. Two express cars were intended to carry packages and freight. (See Appendix E for some of the express car contents.) On the night of the tragedy, a dog was the last living creature pulled from the wreckage, a bull terrier that had been leashed to an express car. Hearing sounds as though human moans, the *Ashtabula Telegraph* newspaper foreman, E. J. Griffin, roped himself and ascended the railcar. Ripping a hole in the metal roof of the car with a spike-hammer, he was able to remove the scorched and bruised dog.

4. Two baggage cars carried passenger luggage.

5. The first passenger coach was for day passengers. At least sixteen persons escaped from it, more than from any other car. Mr. Alfred Parslow, one of the survivors from the car, caught the stove, burning and blistering his hand, while standing in frigid ice-water. Unknown at the time, he also had a piece of gilt molding, one-inch wide, three-quarters of an inch thick, and eight-inches long, projecting through

his left shoulder. He was not even aware of it until he reached safety.

6. The second passenger coach was for day passengers, also. It apparently struck at an angle, was crushed and broken, falling among rods and braces of the bridge, and it appears that no one escaped from it. Approximately forty passengers were in the car. While none survived, passengers' bodies were better preserved since the car fell in the stream at the point where the water was deepest, thus protecting them from the fire. Many ladies were on board.

7. The smoker car was for passengers who smoked. About sixteen persons were in the car. Five were known to have been killed. The stove warming the car fell from one end to the other, making a clean sweep of everything and everyone in its path. The car stood at an angle after the fall. The train's conductor, Bernhart Henn, was in the rear of the smoker when the accident occurred.

8. Yokahama was the drawing-room car, or parlor car. There was only one survivor, since the City of Buffalo sleeper knocked the Yokahama on its side on the way down, and then crushed it through its entire length. P. P. Bliss and wife may have been in the Yokahama.

9. Palatine was the New York sleeper. George A. White, a survivor, said the Palatine "fell as it rode . . . bodily and straight . . . which saved our lives." Mrs. Swift was wedged between two seats in the Palatine. She managed to free herself and checked on her husband who, in the fall, had been hurled across the aisle, was trapped and unconscious so that she thought he was dead. With the aid of Mr. White, she was able to extricate her husband, who regained consciousness, but was delirious. Miss Marion Shepard, Mrs. Anna Graham, and Mr. White then took or assisted everybody out of the car.

10. City of Buffalo was the Boston sleeper car. When it fell, it landed on its forward end, with its rear end high in the air,

resting on the Yokahama and the Palatine. About twenty-one people were in the car, possibly including Mr. and Mrs. P. P. Bliss. The fall probably crushed most passengers, and the position of the car created a draft that intensified the heat and flames. The fire in City of Buffalo was still burning at 2 a.m. Mr. H. A. White of Wethersfield, Connecticut, was one of only three persons to have survived from that car.

11. Osceo was the last car, and was the Louisville sleeper. It was thought there were only three ladies and the porter in the car. The brakeman, A. L. Stone, of Ripley, New York, who survived, testified that at the time of the crash he was in the rear, stateroom section of the Osceo.

The Bridge

Erected in 1865, the bridge that collapsed December 29, 1876 was a wrought-iron Howe truss bridge, 165 feet in total length, 150 feet from abutment to abutment. (Howe truss bridges are still in use today and are quite common in the Pacific Northwest.) The bridge was nineteen-feet wide, with double track, and the Pacific Express was on the south track the night of the accident. From the bottom of the trusses to the top deck where the track was laid was twenty feet. The dead weight of the bridge was three thousand pounds to the square foot. It cost $75,000.

The Ohio Legislature, in its inquiry, judged the safety factor of the bridge to be between 1.2 and 1.6: i.e., the bridge was strong enough to carry 20–60 percent more load than the maximum to which it might actually be subjected at any time.

Theories about Why the Bridge Fell

A thorough discussion of reasons for the bridge failure appears in another essay in this volume. However, a couple of interesting theories are worth noting. One theory is that the cars became derailed so that the wheels were rolling on the flooring of the bridge, causing the flooring to give way and pulling both walls of trusses inward at the top. Another old Ashtabula fable is that the engines were speeding to make up lost time and, when the engineer discovered how close he was to the depot, he locked up the brakes and the downward pressure collapsed the bridge. The Ohio Legislature, after its inquiry involving experts, expressed surprise that the bridge had stood for eleven years.

Railroad Accidents

The railroad was fast becoming commonplace, but many safety features and precautions had yet been put into place in 1876. In 1875, there were at least 1,201 accidents. By 1880, the total was 8,216. Ashtabula's was the worst, but about forty bridges failed during the 1870s. In the 1880s, two hundred railroad bridges failed.

Railroad History

The Cleveland, Painesville and Ashtabula Railroad was chartered February 11, 1848 and began service in 1852. It became the Cleveland and Lake Erie Railroad in 1868 before becoming the Lake Shore and Michigan Southern Railway Company (LS&MS) in 1869, its name at the time of the Ashtabula train-bridge disaster, December 29, 1876. The LS&MS was a Vanderbilt line, part of the empire of Cornelius "Commodore" Vanderbilt. Later, it would be merged into the New York Central System before being subsumed under Conrail.

Conclusion

Though I have had great fun finding artifacts from the Ashtabula bridge disaster, I realize how regrettable it is that so much has been missed. I was too late. Over the years, much valuable material was lent and never returned, sold and scattered to many different states and areas, to people who never realized an object's significance. The stories still abound. An elderly lady related the story her grandfather had told, of playing with a child survivor of the disaster who, immediately after the accident in 1876, stayed at their home, until relatives could come to get him.

The half of an ax I found earlier this year—could it be the ax with which Griffin hacked his way through the railcar roof to rescue the dog? A few years ago, when they tore down the old building that had been the Eagle Hotel, the owner told me there was still blood on the hardwood floors dating back to the 1876 accident. More than 125 years later, the mystery survives.

I was a little late. So many of the people who had knowledge and stories of the accident are gone—and their stories with them. I would love to have had coffee with them and listened to their tales. Maybe that is the way it is supposed to be. It keeps the mystery alive.

Appendices

Appendix A
The Testimony of Some Survivors

Upon impact, many victims, stunned by the cruel surprise of having been hurled into the cold, snowy night, with wreckage and fire all around, instantly assumed they were the only survivors—given the initial silence and devastation of the scene, with only the eerie illumination of the well-fed fires. Sixteen passengers survived in the first day coach. The second day coach had no known survivors. Inside the smoking car, the heating stove ricocheted from one end of the car to the other, making a clean sweep killing four passengers and drove Sleeping Car Conductor Wagner through the end of the car killing him instantly. The Yokahama had only one survivor. Most Palatine passengers survived. Only three from the City of Buffalo lived to tell about it. Of those in the Osceo, Porter James Doyle and perhaps, Mrs. Frank Eastman did not escape death (Peet, 1877).

Mr. Parslow from the first day coach gave this description of his experience:

> The first intimation I had of the affair was the sound of the crash of the bridge. I felt and realized the sensation of the downward tendency of the coach. I clutched one of the seats to steady myself. All of a sudden, in the lash of a second, the passengers were thrown to the end of the coach that had reached the water. The broken pieces of ice, the snow, and fragments of the car came in with a rush. I caught the stove, which had not yet been cooled from its heat, thinking to save myself thereby from drowning. In doing so, I burned my hand to a blister, while the other portion of my body was freezing in the water. I remember the crashing of the smoker upon my car. As soon as I could collect my thoughts, I went to work to extricate myself, but how I did it I'm uncertain. I only know that I found myself out of the car and into the fragments of ice and floating pieces of the wreck. The screams of the dying and crushed broke upon my ears, and were the most pitiful sounds that I've ever heard. I managed to reach unbroken ice and from thence I climbed up the height."

It should be noted that Mr. Parslow had a piece of gilt molding, one-inch wide, three-quarters of an inch thick, and eight-inches long, through his left shoulder. He was not aware of his situation until he reached safety. Mr. Parslow indicated that there were forty to forty-five passengers in his car. He thought the smoking car held the same number. It was his opinion that there were two hundred passengers on the train (Peet, 1877).

Mr. J. M. Earle from the smoking car described his ordeal:

> It did not seem to me as if we had fallen. I was thoroughly collapsed for a minute or two. Then I heard two or three crashes . . . cars tumbling off the bridge and striking ours. At the second crash I threw myself on the floor and crouched down under the seats. I did not know, but the next one would crush us all. There were several people near me, and I told them to crouch down. In the coming down the feeling was a beautiful conglomeration of swimming and swinging. . . . I didn't know whether I was on my head or heels. I can't describe how I felt when the car struck the solid ice. Every part of my body seemed to be going in opposite directions. I did not experience a dead calm, but a feeling of intense agony; and that continued until I came to myself. It must have been half an hour certainly before I knew what I was doing. Then I got up and struggled around. The terrible noise made by the falling cars made me hold my breath when I thought it was about time for another to come down (Peet, 1877).

The survival of Mr. George A. White from the sleeper Palatine was a different experience:

> In going down there was hardly any sound. The only thing we heard was that heavy breathing which bespeaks a fear of something terrible to come. The first sound that greeted my ear was after we struck the ice. The breaking of the glass was like rifle shots, and the train coming down made a terrific roar. Our car fell as it rode . . . bodily and straight . . . which saved our lives. As soon as the car touched bottom I could see nothing, all was dark. I groped my way out through the east end of the car. Behind us was the Buffalo car, standing on end, almost perpendicular, resting against the abutment of the bridge, one end having taken our platform. I think none of the Buffalo car passengers was saved. The coach fell on end, and I never heard a sound from it after the fall, and no one came out. All was death in my estimation. The Buffalo was full of passengers. The parlor

car was just ahead of us, and no one came out of it. I think all the passengers it held were killed. At the right of us, facing the west, a car that lay on its side. The top of it was close onto ours. Our car lay just as it was running. I went up over the roof of the other car to take a look up and around. I saw a gentleman and, I think, a lady, following me. On looking into the car, I saw a large number of people lying together in a mass. The car was crushed at its bottom and sides. The scene within was horrible, heartrending . . . indescribable. It was enough to unnerve the bravest. There were maimed and bruised men, women, and children, all held down by cruel timbers. They were in different stages of delirium and excitement. Some were screaming, some were groaning, and others praying. There was hardly anyone within who seemed rational. I saw the encroachments the fire was making. While on the roof of that car I took a speedy survey of the situation. I realized the terrible, yawning chasm. I shall never forget the horrors of that night (Peet, 1877).

Mr. H. A. White from the sleeper City of Buffalo told his story:

The first thought that came into my mind was that I was dead; that it was no use for me to stir or try to help myself. I waited in that position until I heard two more crashes come, when all was quiet; I then tried to see if I could not raise what was on and around me and succeeded. I opened my eyes and the first thing I saw, was the top of the door that opened into the saloon in the rear end of the car. I struck that immediately with my hand and thrust my head through it. I spoke then. Up to this time there was not a shriek or voice heard in the car that I was in . . . all had been stilled (Peet, 1877).

The news media gave this account of Mrs. Foster Swift's escape from the sleeper Palatine:

Mrs. Swift retained her senses and her presence of mind. She was badly injured at the time, but did not realize it. When the accident occurred, there was a terrible crash; the bell rope snapped like the report of a pistol, and the lights were extinguished. As the cars went down there was no noise. Her husband was hurled across the aisle and held down senseless. She was wedged in between two seats, but extricated herself. She spoke to her husband, but he made no reply, and she thought he was dead. The agony of her mind at that moment was fearful to contemplate. She finally, with the aid of Mr. White, got him out.

He was then delirious, and hardly knew where he was going. Her anxiety was all for her husband. Miss Shepard, Mrs. Graham and Mr. White then took or assisted everybody out of the car, reassuring them by words and deeds, and thus aided in saving many lives (Peet, 1877).

Many of the passengers spoke of Miss Marion Shepard from the sleeper Palatine and regarded her as a heroine in the horrible event. She has been described as being brave, while surrounded by danger, and she acted in a very calm and collected manner. She was described by passenger C. E. Torris as being selfless, dipping her handkerchief in the ice-cold river and washing blood off the face of a wounded man. Even citizens of Ashtabula spoke of her, stating that it was unusual to see her assist the wounded as they lay in the engine house near the station in a calm, deliberate manner. They called her "a good angel" sent to give comfort to those in need. Miss Shepard told her story:

The passengers were grouped about the car in twos, fours, and even larger parties. Some were lunching, some were chatting, and quite a number were playing cards. The bell-rope snapped in two, one piece flying against one of the lamp glasses, smashing it, and knocking the burning candle to the floor. Then the cars ahead of us went bump, bump, bump, as if the wheels were jumping over ties. Until the bumping sensation was felt, everyone thought the glass globe had been broken by an explosion. Several jumped up, and some seized the tops of the seats to steady themselves. Suddenly there was an awful crash. I can't describe the noise. There were all sorts of sounds. I could hear, above all, a sharp, ringing sound, as if all the glass in the train was being shattered in pieces. Someone cried out, 'We're going down!' At that moment all the lights in the car went out. It was utter darkness. I stood up in the centre of the aisle. I knew that something awful was happening, and having some experience in railroad accidents, I braced myself as best I knew how. I felt the car floor sinking under my feet. The sensation of falling was very apparent. I thought of a great many things, and I made up my mind I was going to be killed. For the first few seconds we seemed to be dropping in silence. I could hear the other passengers breathing. Then suddenly the car was filled with flying splinters and dust, and we seemed breathing some heavy substance. For a moment, I was almost suffocated. We went down, down. Oh, it was awful! It seemed to me we had been falling two minutes. The berths were slipping from their fastenings and falling upon the passengers. We heard an awful crash. As the sound died away there were heavy groans all around us. It was as dark as the grave. I was thrown down. Just how I fell is more than I can say. A gentleman had fallen across me, but we were both on our feet in a moment. Everyone alive was scrambling and struggling to get out. I heard someone say, 'Hurry out; the car will be on fire in a minute!' Another man shouted, 'The water is coming in, and we will be drowned!' The car seemed lying partly on one side. In the scramble a man caught hold of me and cried out, 'Help me; don't leave me!' A woman, from one corner of the car, cried, 'Help me save my husband!' He was caught under a berth and some seats. I was feeling around in the dark, trying to release him, when someone at the other end of the car said they were all right and would help the man out. I groped along to the door, crawling over the heating arrangement in getting to it. While I was getting out at the door, others were crawling out the windows. On the left the cars were on fire. On the right a pile of rubbish, as high as I could see, barred escape. In front of me were some cars standing on end, or in a sloping position. I followed a man who was trying to scale the pile of debris. I got up to a coach which was resting on one edge of the roof. The side was so slippery and icy I could not walk on it, and so I crawled over it. The car was dark inside, and oh, what heart rending groans issued from it! It seemed filled with people who were dying. Two men, a Mr. White, of Chicago, and a Mr. Tyler, of St. Louis, helped me down from the end of the car. Then I was in snow up to my knees. Mr. Tyler was badly gashed about the face, and was covered with blood. This stain on my sleeve was blood from his wound. Right under our feet lay a man, his head down in a hole and his legs under the corner of a car. He asked help, and Mr. White and Mr. Tyler released his legs somehow, and some other men carried him away. It was storming terribly. The wind was blowing a perfect gale. By this time, the scene was lighted up by the burning cars. The abutments looked as high as Niagara. Away above us, I could see a crowd of spectators. Down in the wreck there was perfect panic. Some were so badly frightened and panic stricken that they had to be dragged out of the cars to prevent them from burning up. Before we got out of the chasm, the whole train was in a blaze. The locomotive, the cars, and the bridge were mixed up in one indistinguishable mass. From the burning heap came shrieks and the most piteous cries for help. I could hear far above me the clangor of bells, alarming the citizens. We climbed up the deep side of the gorge, floundering in snow two feet deep. They took us to an engine house, where there was a big furnace fire. The wounded were brought in and laid on the floor. They were injured in every conceivable way. Some had their legs broken; some had gashed and bleeding faces; and some were so horribly crushed they seemed to be dying.

Appendix B

[Transcription of the handwritten report of
Dr. Stephen Smith, June 3, 1878, of his examination of the
remains of Charles Collins.]

Report of an Examination of the alledged [sic] Skull of the late Mr. Collins, of Cleveland, Ohio. with Conclusions

On the 26th day of April, 1878, I carefully examined a skull certified to be that of the late Mr. Collins, of Cleveland, Ohio, formerly Chief Engineer of the Lake Shore and Michigan Southern Rail Road.

The following were the main noticeable features of that skull observed at that examination.

I. The Skull
   1. The skull was of medium size, the measurements being as follows—from central point of ear to ear, directly over the vertex, twelve & three-fourths inches; from the same points over the parietal eminences, thirteen and one-half inches; from the occipital protuberance to the nasal eminence of the frontal bone eleven inches.
   2. The bones of the skull are all unusually thin, being generally translucent and at points almost transparent.
   3. The calvarium had been removed in the usual manner, with a saw, and on a line with the occipital protuberance and the orbital ridges.
   4. The orbital plates of the frontal bone are of extreme thinness, being scarcely more than a line in thickness.

II. The Openings

5. An irregular opening is found in the left orbital plate, about half an inch in its longest diameter, the margins of which are very sharp & at points, angular. A similar opening is found in the right orbital plate, but longer and narrower, with extremely thin margins.

6. A hole is found in the left parietal bone, about three-fourths of an inch posterior to the parietal eminences, it is four inches from the left meatus auditorius externus, its diameter is about one half inch; it is slightly oval in form in the perpendicular direction; the external margins are cleanly cut, except at the upper edge where the external table is chipped off leaving minute traces of lead as is proved by testing with the Nélaton probe. On the inside the internal table is found broken away at several point & at the upper margin is beveled off, as if by a blunt instrument, so as to make a deep groove extending one fourth of an inch, in a direction towards the center of the vortex. This groove has tracings of lead which are readily disclosed by the eye.

7. A large irregular opening is found on the left side of the cranium, two & one half inches in length antero-posteriorly and one and a half inches in breadth, vertically; the center is five inches from the right meatus auditorius externus, and one and a half inches from the longitudinal fracture on the vertex. This opening is exactly filled by properly adjusting several fragments of bone with the exception of one small space, which I am informed was accurately filled by a fragment of bone which has recently been mislaid. In order to adjust these fragments they had to be placed together protruding externally, roof-like. When the opening was then closed, the external and internal surfaces presented a uniformly smooth

surface, without any chipping or beveling off as noticeable in and around the hold on the left side. On examining the margins of these bones it is apparent that they were driven outward.

III. The Fractures

8. From the left hole two fractures proceed. (a) downwards obliquely in the direction of a point midway between the mastoid process and the occipital protuberance, about one-fourth of an inch, where it divides into three fractures. (b)passing directly forwards creating a fine fissure, two and one-half inches in length. (c)downwards and forwards to the temporal fossa, five inches in length. (d) directly backwards to the occipital suture, three inches in length. The second main fracture (e)runs upwards to the vertex, in an oblique direction towards the center of the right opening, one and a half inches, where it terminates after inclining directly forwards, in a fracture (f)running transversely over the vertex; on the left this fracture runs half an inch, then turns at a right angle and runs forward to the coronal suture, as firm suture. The right branch of (f)runs one fourth of an inch, and near the saggital suture divides, one branch (g)continues in a straight line with the main fracture down to the junction of the parietal with the temporal bone, with two fissures extending backwards one nearly to the occipito-parietal (lambdoidal) suture. The other branch of the (f), (h), runs forward on the left side of the saggital suture, nearly to the junction of the saggital with the coronal suture where crosses to the rightside, passes across the frontal bone towards the right orbit, and as the orbital eminence it curves around to the right side & ends as a fissure at the junction of the frontal and right temporal bones. Near the point where this

fracture crosses the saggital sutures a broad fracture (m) commences on its left side and passes at right angles to the right, one and one half inches and terminates in the middle of the right opening. On the opposite side of this hole another another [sic] fracture (n) is found running backwards and downwards, and terminates in the fissure which runs from the vertex, or (i).

Conclusions

A careful examination of these openings and fractures, and of their relations, combined with experiments, justify the following Conclusions:

I. They are shot injuries. This is proved by the nature of the left hole which is nearly round, and clearly cut, and marked by lead on its external and internal margins.

II. The left opening was made by the entrance of the ball – This is proved by the comparatively clean cut edges of the external table, and the beveling of the internal margins by the chipping off of the internal table for a considerable extent.

III. The right opening was made by the ball in its exit, or attempted exit. This is proved by the large size of the opening and the method of adjustment of the fragments which requires that they should be first arranged so as to present externally, showing that the violence was applied from within outwardly, thus protruding them externally.

IV. The ball which entered the left hole escaped at the right, or fell backward into the cavity after causing the fracture. This is proved by the direction of the track of the ball, and of the line of fracture. The track of the ball is marked by a groove on the inner table at the upper angle of the left hole, with slight breaking of the external table at the same point. The bearing of this track or groove is in direct line with the centre of the right opening. The fractures are of two kinds, one central and broad, the others radiating as fissures. The main or central fracture runs obliquely from the lower angle of the left opening downwards about one fourth of an inch where it radiates as fissures in three directions. This part of the central fracture was made by the first impact of the ball on the lower margin of the hole. The second central fracture begins at the opposite or upper angle of the hole and taking a zigzag direction terminates in the right opening. This irregularity of direction is due to differences of frangibility of the portions of the different bones which it transverses. One branch of this central fracture continues beyond the right hole down to the lower margin of the right orbital border of the frontal.

Experiments—In the several experiments made with a navy revolver eleven inches in length, seven shooter, it was uniformly found that when a ball entered the skull at the left opening & in the direction marked by the groove, struck the inside of the skull at a point corresponding with the centre of the right opening, and either fractured the bones outwardly, and escaped, or fell back into the cavity of the skull. In every case a broad central fractured [sic] was found extending from the left to the right opening, in a zigzag direction, with fissures branching at various points, and a continuation of the central fracture beyond the right opening through the right half of the frontal bone.

V. The ball was cylindro-conoidal. This is proved by the nature of the two openings. The hole made by the entrance of the ball is clean cut on the external surface except at the upper margin where the internal table is grooved which corresponds with the holes made in the skull by the conoidal ball. The right opening consists of a number of fragments upheaved by a broad missile which corresponds with the effects of cylindrical balls which have lost their balance, or direction in the line of the long diameter, and now present the nick to the opposing bones of the skull, and necessarily create a large breach.

VI. The ball was deflected from its course and may have fallen back into the brains, or, if it escaped, have passed out at a considerable angle. This is proved by the fact that balls entering the cavity of the skull often break through the opposite walls and then fall back, and are found in the brain, or when they escape are deflected to a degree depending upon the nature of the resistance. The direction of the escaping body was nearly at right angles with the point where it impinged upon the internal wall as appears when the fragments are placed in situ. The same results were obtained in experiments, viz. Deflection of the ball when it struck the wall opposite so as to escape nearly at right angles with first course, and then either breaking through and falling back, or escaping through the scalp. But it is alledged [sic] that in the case of Mr. Collins there was an opening in the scalp on the right side, which proves that the ball did escape. This statement is probably true. Owing to the extreme thinness of the skull at this point the resistance to the ball was not very great.

VII. The muzzle of the weapon was held at a distance of not less than four inches from the skull. This is proved by the escape of the ball from the skull. Experiments proved that when the muzzle is held close to the skull the ball does not escape, even in thin skulls, but makes more or less impression on the opposite wall, continues fracturing it extending, [sic] & even making a hole sufficiently large to allow it to escape, but even then not perforating the scalp, but falling back into the brain. It is only when this muzzle is held at a distance of four or more inches from the skull that the ball acquires sufficient momentum to pass out of the skull and scalp, & lodge at some distance from the hand.

VIII. The openings in the orbital plates of the frontal bone were due to sudden impulse of the brain. This explanation is in accordance with that given by high authority (Prof. _____) in the case of similar lesions in the skull of President Lincoln who received a pistol shot wound in very nearly the same direction as the late Mr. Collins.

IX. The wound did not prove immediately fatal. This is proved by the fact that it did not involve vital parts of the brain, nor large blood vessels. The history of similar shot wounds shows that persons frequently do not even become unconscious, but die many days after from inflammation of the structures involved. But where unconsciousness immediately ensues, life is still prolonged several hours, and the patient is either quiet from paralysis, or restless and excited from irritation of the injured brain tissue.

Additional Facts

In connection with the preceding examination the following well authenticated facts must have due importance given them in arriving at final Conclusions:

1. Mr. Collins was right handed.
2. The body was found in the bed where he was accustomed to sleep several days after he disappeared, and in a state of incipient decomposition.
3. His clothes lay on a chair precisely as he was accustomed to place them.
4. The body lay in bed in a very natural position, the clothes being smoothly drawn up to the axillae ["armpits"].
5. The left arm lay on the outside of the clothes the hand resting on the inside of the left thigh, with the hilt of a navy revolver lying loosely in it, this pistol was eleven inches in length, a six shooter, and three chambers were empty. Near it on the

clothes was a razor, and Derringer pistol fully loaded.

6. The head was turned to the left side and there were two wounds in the scalp corresponding to the openings in the skull. The pillow and bed were saturated with blood.

6. [sic] In the mahogany head board there was a dent, and in the wood work of a closet at the right of the bed was another dent, and on the floor just below the latter was a ball much flattened.

7. The two pistols were recognized as belonging to the deceased; the navy pistol as usually kept under the mattress on the left side of where he always slept, and the Derringer was placed under his wife's pillow for convenience in case of assault.

General Conclusions

The preceding facts properly collated and arranged justify the conclusion that this was not a case of suicide. The place of entrance of the ball, the position of the left hand partially enclosing the handle of the pistol, the undisturbed state of the body and of the bed-clothes, are entirely inconsistent with the theory of suicide for the following reasons:

1. A right-handed man, however dextrous, could not without the greatest effort, and by placing his hand in the most constrained position, and strongly everting his head, have brought the muzzle of a revolver eleven inches in length to bear upon the point of entrance of the ball in the direction which it took. And even if he had accomplished that feat he must have pressed the muzzle firmly against the scalp to have maintained its position—an inference disproved by the examination of the skull.

2. Experience proves that wounds of this kind may result in 1. Shock without loss of consciousness; 2. Shock and unconsciousness with cerebral irritation; 3. Paralysis, and not immediate death. None of these conditions are consistent with the theory of suicide: – for –

    (a) If there had been shock and unconsciousness, the suicide would not have composed himself, and remained quiet in bed until he died of inflammation. On the contrary, he would either have inflicted other wounds with the weapons at his command, or have relented and sought relief for the wound already inflicted and from which he was suffering severely.

(b) If there were shock and unconsciousness, without paralysis, the cerebral irritation would have caused various contortions of all the limbs and have terminated in violent spasms.

(c) If there had been instant paralysis the pistol would have fallen from the hand, and the hand would have fallen from the side off the bed in the state of extreme abduction of the arm at the moment.

(d) In any event, if the wound was suicidal, the muzzle resting against the scalp, the recoil of the weapon would have been such as to have thrown it some distance from the bed. From a careful analysis of all the facts presented, aided by experience in the investigation of suicidal and homicidal wounds of the head, and experiments with weapons similar to those supposed to have been employed, my opinion is that Mr. Collins came to his death by a shot wound inflicted by other hands than his own.

> Stephen Smith, M.D.
> Surgeon to Bellair and
> St. Vincent's Hospitals, New York
> Prof. of Surgical Jurisprudence
> University Medical
> College, New York

New York. June, 3, 1878 –

Appendix C
*[Transcription of the handwritten report of
Dr. Frank H. Hamilton, June, 1878, upon his examination
of the remains of Charles Collins.]*

Case of Mr. Collins

I – Facts assumed as proven

It will be assumed that, if Mr. Collins took his own life, the act was committed after much formal preparation —that the weapon employed was the navy revolver found in his left hand—that the ball entered at the opening found in the skull back of the center of the left parietal bone, & emerged through the right parietal bone near the coronal suture, & that he was not left-handed.

It will be assumed, also, that his left arm & hand were found lying parallel to his body, or nearly so—the hand partly over and across the thigh, with the weapon lying loosely in his hand—that the right arm was in a similar position in relation to the right side of his body—that the bedclothes were drawn up to a point above the waist; that his legs were extended, and that his whole body was in a condition of easy & natural repose.

II – Argument

The following constitute serious objections to the theory of suicide under the conditions above assumed:

1st. It is highly improbable that a man who is not left-handed would use his left hand in shooting himself in the head, especially when the act was a matter of careful deliberation, forethought & study; —when nothing interfered with the use of the right hand; —when the weapon employed was a navy revolver, eleven & half inches in length and weighing as much as this weighed.

2d. It would, in fact, be exceedingly difficult for a man, not left handed, to hold such a weapon, with his left hand, in the position in which it must have been held for the ball to take the course which it did take, and it would have been impossible for him to have held it steadily, & to have aimed it correctly at a portion of his head where he could not see the exact direction of the muzzle, unless he had rested it against the skull, and especially would it have been impossible for him to have held the weapon so steadily & so firmly that the barrel would not have been thrown out of line, when he pulled the trigger, unless the muzzle rested against the scalp.

3d. Whether the weapon was held firmly against the scalp, or more or less removed, the left arm & hand would not probably have been found in the position in which they were found, with the weapon lying loose in the hand: and for the following reasons:—

The wound was a fatal one and the patient was rendered immediately insensible, & was more or less paralyzed; and if so, his heavy weapon, held with his left arm at a right angle with his body, & to a great disadvantage, would have fallen from his grasp beside his head, and his arm would have fallen off to the left & probably over the side of the bed. If, however, the paralysis of the arm & hand was not complete, and the hand still retained its grasp upon the weapon, both would have fallen off to the left over the side of the bed; or, if the hand could have descended to the position in which it was found being carried there by muscular action, & not by the force of gravity, thus indicating that he still retained nervous & muscular power, the fact that he retained such power after the injury was inflicted, would have been indicated by the displacement of his right hand (convulsive), & there would not have been such a condition of repose & order in his person and bed clothes as was actually found.

If the patient recovered his consciousness more or less completely after a time—a supposition which is scarcely possible, considering the nature and character of his injuries, and the fact that he died very soon—but if he did recover somewhat, he was certainly dazed as consciousness began to return, & would certainly have disturbed his bed clothes to say the least, &

probably would not have been found in his bed. If he recovered completely— which is still less possible—he would probably have resorted at once to those other weapons which were apparently provided for such a contingency; or in case he had repented of his act, there would have been left unmistakable signs of a struggle for life and for succor.

In short, if Mr. Collins was rendered immediately unconscious & was completely paralyzed, & remained so until death, (which was probably the fact) the position of the left arm, & hand, & of the revolver is not satisfactorily explained, upon the theory of suicide. If some power to hold the weapon continued from the first, the position in which they were found is not explained, and the repose of other parts is not explained satisfactorily. If he recovered partially, the general condition of repose is not explained. If he recovered consciousness completely every thing remains unexplained.

All the conditions known, & named above, can only be rendered consistent with themselves, by supposing that Mr. Collins left arm & hand, & the revolver, were arranged & disposed after death.

III – Conclusions

The facts in this case are utterly irreconcilable with the theory of suicide while they do not present the shadow of an objection to the theory that his life was taken by another person while he was lying asleep in his bed, that the shot rendered him at once unconscious, causing complete paralysis of this entire body, — that he never recovered from the unconsciousness or paralysis & that after his death, which took place speedily owing to the profuse hemorrhage, his left arm & hand with the revolver, were placed in the position in which they were found.

Frank H. Hamilton M.D.
June 1878

Appendix D

Editor's Note: On a train in 1876, there was no passenger manifest and not even a reliable method of assuring the number of persons on the train at any given time. Frequent stops allowed local passengers ingress and egress. As a result, no one has ever been able to establish the actual number of persons on the Ashtabula train the night of December 29, 1876. Therefore, the number of survivors and of those killed has never been firmly established. The *Ashtabula Telegraph* for February 4, 1877, quotes Charles Paine, general superintendent of the Lake Shore and Michigan Southern Railway Company as saying the train included seventy-two adults and eight children for a total of eighty fatalities; sixty-nine were saved, although some were still doubtful at the time, and we know that at least one additional person died after that report. The *Ashtabula News* (February 14, 1877), a little more than a week later, claimed that eighty-two persons had been "supposed lost," and the same issue reported the death of yet an additional person, H. T. Tomlinson.

It was noted that the railroad company had made "voluntary and satisfactory settlements" with 139 out of 156 claimants, who were either injured themselves or lost friends or family in the accident. It was claimed that there were "seventeen persons with whom adjustments have not yet been made, some of whom sustained no injuries and claim no damages" (*History of Ashtabula County 1798–1878*).

The monument in Chestnut Grove Cemetery, installed nineteen years after the accident, but while many survivors, rescuers, and public officials were still alive, acknowledges the burial of bodies or body parts or effects representing nineteen additional persons unnamed. Therefore, it would seem that some who lost their lives in the accident have never been identified, and their names have never been confirmed as victims of the accident.

The rosters below have been checked and rechecked against available news reports, and contemporary sources, and are believed to be the most complete listings ever published.

Survivors

1. Mabel Arnold, North Adams, MA
2. Ellen Austin, Omaha, NE (See Appendix I.)
3. Mary Austin, Omaha, NE (See Appendix I.)
4. R. Austin, Chicago, IL
5. Louis Beauchate, Kent's Plains, CT
6. Mrs. Minerva Bingham, Chicago, IL
7. Mrs. William Harrison Bradley, Chicago, IL
8. H. L. Brewster, Milwaukee, WI
9. J. E. Burchell, Chicago, IL
10. A. Burnham, Milwaukee, WI
11. Charles A. Carter, Brooklyn, NY
12. H. D. Champlain, Cleveland, OH
13. D. H. Clark, Westfield, MA
14. Frank L. Collier, Elmira, NY
15. George Covey, Buffalo, NY
16. Mrs. T. A. Davis, Kokomo, IN (See Appendix I.)
17. Cornelius de Maranville, Greenbush, NY
18. James M. Dean, Parker, IN
19. William Dinan, Niagara Falls, NY
20. J. M. Earle, Chicago, IL
21. Mrs. Frank Eastman
22. G. D. "Pap" Folsom, Cleveland, OH
23. Andrew Gibson, Carey, OH
24. Mrs. Anna Graham, New York City, NY
25. Dr. C. A. Griswold, Fulton, IL
26. Ettie Hamlin, Lafayette, IN
27. Richard Harold, Cincinnati, OH
28. Walter Hayes, Lexington, KY
29. J. B. Hazleton, Charleston, IL
30. Bernhart Henn, Buffalo, NY
31. A. E. Hewitt, Bridgeport, CT
32. Alexander Hitchcock, Port Clinton, OH
33. James F. Hunt, Erie, PA
34. [Mr.]_____ Hyderman, Albany, NY (See Appendix I.)
35. Thomas J. Jackson, Waterbury, CT
36. C. E. Jones, Beloit, WI
37. John J. Lalor, Chicago, IL
38. Mrs. W. H. Lew, Rochester, NY

39. P. B. Lewellen, Parker, IN
40. F. W. Lobdell, Troy, NY
41. B. B. Lyons, New York City, NY
42. A. Maillard, San Rafael, CA
43. Judson M. Martin, East Avon, NY
44. Mrs. Judson M. Martin, East Avon, NY
45. Martin son, East Avon, NY
46. Martin daughter, East Avon, NY
47. R. S. McGee, Cleveland, OH
48. Dan McGuire, Erie, PA
49. Alexander Monroe, Somerville, MA
50. Robert Monroe, Rutland, MA
51. J. M. Mowry, Hartford, CT
52. Johnson B. Orburn, Saginaw County, MI (See Appendix I.)
53. Mrs. Johnson B. Orburn, Saginaw County, MI (See Appendix I.)
54. F. A. Ormsbee, Boston, MA
55. Franklin Osborn, Tecumseh, MI
56. Alfred H. Parslow, Chicago, IL
57. Charles D. Patterson, Chicago, IL
58. George M. Reed, Cleveland, OH
59. Charles C. Rickard, Biddeford, ME
60. William B. Sanderson, Auburn, ME
61. Bernard Sawyer, Chesterfield, NY
62. Burritt B. Seymour, Ashtabula, OH
63. Henry W. Shepard, Brooklyn, NY
64. Miss Marion Shepard, Ripon, WI
65. Jerry Stewart, Chicago, IL
66. A. L. Stone, Ripley, NY
67. L. B. Sturges, Minneapolis–St. Paul, MN
68. Foster E. Swift, North Adams, MA.
69. Mrs. Foster E. Swift, North Adams, MA
70. Joseph A. Thompson, Wales via Oakland, CA
71. Harvey Tilden, Cleveland, OH
72. Edward Truworthy, Oakland, CA
73. C. H. Tyler, St. Louis, MO
74. W. H. Vosburgh, Buffalo, NY
75. George A. White, Portland, ME
76. Henry A. White, Wethersfield, CT
77. John J. White, Boston, MA
78. Thomas C. Wright, Nashville, TN

Lost and Missing

	Name	Age	Gender	Marital Status	Residence	Occupation	Unrecognized
1	Alby, Thomas	–	M	–	Murfeesboro, TN	–	
2	Aldrich, Joseph H.	–	M	–	Des Moines, IA		Yes
3	Barnard, Louis J.	–	M	Married	Buffalo, NY	Merchant	Yes
4	Birchard, Mary	40	F	Single	Fayetteville, VT (cousin of Ohio Gov. Hayes)	–	
5	Bliss, Lucy Young	35	F	Married	Rome, PA		Yes
6	Bliss, Philip Paul	38	M	Married	Rome, PA	Hymn Composer	Yes
7	Bradley, infant (Mrs. Wm. H. Bradley's Child)	Inf	–	Single	Chicago, IL	–	Yes
8	Brunner, Charles E.	–	M	Married	Gratiot, WI	Merchant	Yes
9	Brunner, Mrs. C. E. (Mattie)	–	F	Married	Gratiot, WI	Housewife	Yes
10	Brunner, (daughter of C. E. – Lotti)		F	Single	Gratiot, WI	–	Yes
11	Brunner, (son of C. E. – Henry)		M	Single	Gratiot, WI		Yes
12	Caine, Charles (or Kane)	–	M		Pittsburgh, PA	LS&MS Porter	
13	Campbell, D. (nephew of Mrs. Fonda)		M	Married	Milledgeville, IL	–	
14	Campbell, John R.	–	M		–	–	Yes
15	Chamberlain, Hiram	55	M	Married	Cuba, NY	Merchant	
16	Chittenden, David	–	M	Married	Cleveland, OH	Billposter	Yes

Name	Age	Gender	Marital Status	Residence	Occupation	Unrecognized
17 Clemens, William	54	M	–	Bellevue, OH	–	
18 Coffin, Mrs. Emeline (daughter of Mrs. Truworthy)	24	F	Married	Oakland, CA	–	Yes
19 Cogswell, M. P.	–	M	Married	Chicago, IL	–	
20 Cook, Mrs. E.	–	F	Married	Wellington, OH	–	
21 Crain, Lewis C.	–	M	Married	West Haven, CT	Traveling Agt.	
22 Cramer, J. C.	–	M	–	Gloversville, NY	–	Yes
23 Crimp, J. E.	–	M	Married	Somerville, MA	Merchant	
24 Doyle, James	–	M	Single	New York City, NY	LS&MS Porter	
25 Fonda, Sarah	80	F	Married	Schuylerville, NY	–	
26 Frame, Mary	36	F	Married	Rochester, NY	–	
27 Frame, (child of Mary Frame)	8	–	Single	Rochester, NY	–	
28 Frame, William (child of Mary Frame)	–	M	Single	Rochester, NY	–	
29 Gage, Clarence N.	–	M	Married	Charleston, IL	Traveling Agt.	
30 George, Mrs. W. J.	–	F	Married	Cleveland, OH	–	
31 George, Mattie (granddaughter of Mrs. W. J.)	–	F	Single	Cleveland, OH	–	
32 Gilley, Alfred (cousin of Mr. Truworthy)–	–	M	–	Cranberry Island, ME	–	
33 Hale, D. T.	–	–	–	Charleston, IL	–	
34 Hall, Mrs. Henry L.	–	F	Married	Chicago, IL	–	Yes
35 Hall, Henry L.	–	M	Married	Chicago, IL	–	Yes
36 Hart, Levi W.	40	M	Married	Akron, OH	Traveling Agt.	

Name	Age	Gender	Marital Status	Residence	Occupation	Unrecognized
37 Hodgkins, Frank A.	23	M	–	Bangor, ME	–	Yes
38 Holdridge, D. M.	–	–	Married		–	Yes
39 Hopkins, Dr. A. W.	–	M	–	Hartland Four Corners, VT	Physician	Yes
40 Hubbard, Dr. George Francis	45	M	Married	Polk City, IA	Physician	
41 Kepler, George W.	29	M	Married	Ashtabula, OH	Merchant	Yes
42 Ketlerville, Annie (or Ketterwall, Kitterville)	13	F	Married	Beloit, WI	Housekeeper	
43 Knowles, Mrs. H. M.	–	F	Married	Cleveland, OH	–	
44 Knowles, (child of Mrs. H. M.)	–	F	Single	Cleveland, OH	–	Yes
45 Koppler, Elizabeth	–	F	Married	Chippewa, Ont, Can	–	
46 Lannegan, Lawrence	22	M	–	Cleveland, OH	Express Asst.	
47 Lewis, Maggie L.	17	F	Single	St. Louis, MO	LS&MS	
48 Livenbroe, Peter	–	M	–	Cleveland, OH	Locomotive Fireman	
49 Mann, Sarah S.	–	F	Single	Cleveland, OH	–	
50 Marston, Mrs. C. M.	–	F	Married	Waterbury, ME	–	Yes
51 Marston, Mrs. J. D.	–	F	Married	Chicago, IL	–	Yes
52 Marston, (child of Mrs. J. D.)	–	F	Single	Chicago, IL	–	Yes
53 Marvin, Fredrick W.	–	M	–	Clayton, MI	–	Yes
54 McNeil, Philip	–	M	Married	Cleveland, OH	LS&MS Baggagemaster	Yes
55 Merrill, S. H.	–	M	Married	Dayton, NY	Merchant	
56 Meyer, Birdie	5	F	Single	Cleveland, OH	–	

	Name	Age	Gender	Marital Status	Residence	Occupation	Unrecognized
57	Meyer, Isaac	–	M	Married	Cleveland, OH	Merchant	Yes
58	Mixer, Minnie	–	F	Single	Buffalo, NY	–	Yes
59	Moore, Mrs. W. L.	74	F	Married	Hammondsport, NY	–	
60	Myers, Libbie (See Appendix I.)	–	F	Married	Buffalo, NY	Milliner	
61	Nusbaum, Victor Lewis	–	M	Single	Cleveland, OH	Merchant	Yes
62	Osborn, Richard	–	M	–	Tecumseh, MI	Farmer	
63	Packard, Mary H.	–	M	Single	West Bridgewater, MA	–	
64	Palmer, Mrs. G. E.	–	F	Married	Binghamton, NY	–	
65	Pickering, Charles R. (nephew of J.D.)	6	M	Single	Chicago, IL	–	
66	Pickering, John D.	22	M	Single	Chicago, IL	Clerk	Yes
67	Potter, John	–	M	–	Painesville, OH	–	Yes
68	Purington, George A.	36	M	–	Buffalo, NY	Express Messenger	Yes
69	Rice, Jonathan	–	M	Married	Lowell, MA	Retired Merchant	Yes
70	Rogers, Dr. Daniel A.	–	M	Single	Chicago, IL	Physician	Yes
71	Rogers, E. P.	–	M	Single	Chicago, IL	–	
72	Rogers, Henry G.	–	M	Married	Springfield, OH	Public School Superintendent	Yes
73	Rogers, Mrs. Henry G.	–	F	Married	Springfield, OH	Housekeeper	Yes
74	Rossiter, Charles	6	M	–	Chicago, IL	–	Yes
75	Russell, Boyd L.	30	M	Married	Auburn, NY	Traveling Agt.	
76	Shattuck, O. Frederick	43	M	–	Millersburg, OH	Mt. Vernon & Delaware RR	Yes

	Name	Age	Gender	Marital Status	Residence	Occupation	Unrecognized
77	Smith, Charlotte N. (sister of Martha)	–	F	Single	Roundout, NY	–	Yes
78	Smith, Martha Ann (sister of Charlotte)	–	F	Single	Roundout, NY	–	Yes
79	Smith, J. W.	–	M	–	Toronto, Ont, Can	Printing Agent	
80	Spooner, George H.	–	M	–	Petersham, MA	–	Yes
81	Steindal, Robert	40	M	Married	New York City, NY	Traveling Agt.	
82	Stockwell, Albert H.	49	M	Married	Ashtabula, OH	Traveling Agt. LS&MS	Yes
83	Stow, Garwood B.	45	M	Married	Geneva, OH	Carpenter	
84	Thayer, Clara J.	–	F	Single	Springfield, MA	Nurse of Mrs. Wm. H. Bradley	Yes
85	Thomas, Mrs. Lucy C.	40	F	Married	Buffalo, NY	–	
86	Thomas, Willie (son of Lucy)	–	M	Single	Buffalo, NY	–	
87	Thomas, W. W.	–	M	Married	Cleveland, OH	Merchant	
88	Tomlinson, H. T.	–	M	–	Bridgeport, CT	–	
89	Truworthy, Mrs. Emeline	–	F	Married	Oakland, CA	–	
90	Unknown (African American)	–	–	–	–	–	Yes
91	Unknown (African American)	–	–	–	–	–	Yes
92	Vogel, Charles	36	M	Married	Albany, NY	Merchant	Yes
93	Volk, Martha Tolita	15	F	Single	Rochester, NY	School Girl	
94	Wagner, Harry	–	M	Married	Syracuse, NY	LS&MS Sleeping Car Conductor	Yes

Name	Age	Gender	Marital Status	Residence	Occupation	Unrecognized
95 Waite, S. D.	30	M	Married	Toledo, OH	U.S. Express Messenger	
96 Washburn, Rev. Dr. Alvan H.	50	M	Married	Cleveland, OH	Minister LS&MS	Yes
97 Webb, James	–	M	–	Philadelphia, PA	Porter	
98 Wilson, William F.	38	M	Single	Boston, MA	Merchant	Yes

Some Unconfirmed

A list of persons not on the official roster, but thought to have been on the train; yet, no identification or personal effects could ever establish whether they were on the train at the time of the disaster, and apparently no statement in print contradicts the possibility that they were passengers when the accident occurred.

Name	Evidence
1. H. J. Clark (Cleveland)	*Ashtabula Telegraph* (January 5, 1877) listed him as one of those "lost."
2. J. O. Hart (West Farmington, OH)	Listed among the deceased in *Ashtabula Telegraph* (January 5, 1877).
3. Mr. Hayden	"Mr. Hayden, perhaps the only man who escaped from the wreck without a single injury" (*The Terrible Ashtabula Railroad Calamity,* p. 6).
4. Mr. and Mrs. J. D. Peck	Names appeared and condition (Peoria, IL) described as "doubtful" in *Ashtabula Telegraph* (January 5, 1877). Listed as deceased in *Ashtabula Sentinel* (January 4, 1877). Also listed among the dead in *The Terrible Ashtabula Railroad Calamity* (p. 7).
5. N. L. Quinby	*Ashtabula News* (February 28, 1877) reported that the former Ashtabulan may have been on the train. He was "last heard of" at Dunkirk, NY, and was expected in Ashtabula at about the time of the accident. No word had been heard since the accident.

Name	Evidence
6. Lewis E. Reynolds	Listed among the dead in *Ashtabula Telegraph* (January 5, 1877).
7. C. E. Torris	Cited as a survivor in Peet's book, *The Ashtabula Disaster.*

Appendix E
A Miscellany More Than 125 Years Later
Thomas E. Corts

1. Resources for Study of the Disaster

As significant as the Ashtabula train-bridge disaster proved to be, it is difficult to believe that no more detailed record exists. We are forever indebted to the work of the Reverend Stephen D. Peet, former minister of Ashtabula's Congregational Church, for his volume, *The Ashtabula Disaster,* first published in 1877. Peet had been trained as an anthropologist and must have recognized the historical importance of the event. With pastoral concern, he interviewed almost every person who survived the accident and apparently worked prodigiously to produce an accurate list of those known to have perished.

Peet was secretary of the American Anthropological Association and editor of the *Quarterly of American Antiquities* (*Ashtabula Sentinel,* January 11, 1877). The newspaper reported at the time, Peet, "has been on the scene of the disaster on the first night, and has been there very

148

much of the time since. He has visited and interviewed all the survivors. His work of gathering antiquities peculiarly fitted him for the work of this terrible emergency. He has made out a careful report of all that can be ascertained thus far, and expects in due time to ascertain the names of every person upon the fated train" (*Ashtabula Sentinel,* January 11, 1877). True to his word, as documented at the time "Peet expects to put all in pamphlet form" (*Ashtabula Sentinel,* January 18, 1877), his book came out in 1877, providing the best detail of the town of Ashtabula at the time, and of the terrible wreck and its victims. First copies arrived in Ashtabula the week of February 21, 1877, approximately eight weeks after the accident. The *News* (February 21, 1877) described the volume as "in very nice style, and in a large edition. . . . It will undoubtedly be eagerly sought for and very interesting as well as a valuable memorial of the great calamity." In his rush to press, certain inaccuracies in names and details appear.

Often overlooked as a resource for study of the Ashtabula train-bridge disaster is the *Memoirs of Philip P. Bliss,* edited by Daniel W. Whittle. While the volume clearly centers on Philip Paul Bliss and his wife, it includes considerable information assembled in one source concerning the city, the train wreck, and its circumstances. Whittle was the ex-Union soldier, who became a prominent businessman, treasurer of the Elgin Watch Co., at a young age before devoting himself to full-time evangelism. Whittle had teamed up with Bliss, and the two had spent a couple of years working closely, side-by-side, as traveling evangelists. They came to know each other well, spending major blocks of time together, and taking mutual responsibility for special services attracting large crowds, cultivating a sense of admiration and respect for one another.

When the accident occurred, evangelist D. L. Moody dispatched Whittle, along with two of his most trusted associates: B. F. Jacobs, a business partner of J. E. Burchell, who was on the train and survived, and was the first to telegraph Whittle, Moody, and Chicago friends of the loss of the Blisses; John V. Farwell, wealthy owner of a large Chicago drygoods store and staunch Moody supporter. They were in Ashtabula by Sunday following the disaster and spent three sad and fruitless days seeking the remains or any identifiable personal effects of the Blisses.

Though drawing upon Bliss's personal diary and his correspondence, Whittle's volume is less a personal memoir than a chronicle of Bliss's life and work. In reporting Bliss's tragic end, Whittle has quoted extensively from survivors and from newspaper and periodical accounts that provide helpful insights. For example, it is Whittle, himself, who pretty well scotches the rumor that has persisted over the years, namely, that Bliss saved himself from the wreckage, and went back into the inferno to die with his wife and children. Burchell had thought he had seen Bliss and family, but was obviously mistaken, inasmuch as Bliss's children were not accompanying them. Another interesting contemporary publication was *The Terrible Ashtabula Railroad Calamity, on the Evening of December 29th 1876, Together with a Few Incidents of P. P. Bliss, the Immortal Singer.* It was published by A. S. Benner in 1877. While more a Gospel tract than an historical account, it includes some names and incidents of note.

Concerning resources for study of the disaster, a great mystery is what happened to the promised volume of J. M. Goodwin, C. E.? Advertisements appeared in the Ashtabula papers of January and February, 1877, following the accident, stating:

> Will appear promptly upon the conclusion of the Investigation A Complete Official Report of the Testimony Taken by A Coroner's Jury Convened Dec. 30th, 1876 at Ashtabula, O., in the Case Arising Out of the Failure of the

Railway Bridge at that Place, Dec. 29th, 1876. Printed by authority, from the notes of the sworn stenographer to the Coroner and Jury; with maps of the railway station grounds, and of the village of Ashtabula; and several views and drawings, showing the wrecked bridge, generally and in detail, and illustrating the statements of experts, witnesses before the Jury. Royal octavo, about 450 pages with plates. Edited by J. M. Goodwin, C. E., Mem. Am Soc. C. E. Railway expert and Associate Council to the Jury, to whom orders for the book may be addressed at Cleveland, Ohio. Price $3.00.

February 21, 1877, the *Ashtabula News* reported it had received a letter from Mr. Goodwin saying he was compelled to give up the publication "on account of the great cost beyond any probable return." The *News*, concluding that the book ought to be published, added:

We are not willing to publish the book at our own expense, but are ready to do so if there are any parties sufficiently interested to guarantee the cost.

The remarkable collection of materials, maintained by the Jennie Munger Gregory Memorial Museum at Geneva-on-the-Lake, Ohio, has been a vital source unknown to most people for many years. The sheaf of contemporary letters, notes, and records, as well as newspapers is a treasure trove for re-examining the Ashtabula train-bridge disaster. Records in the Ohio Room of the Ashtabula Public Library are very helpful in showing how the disaster has been described and treated in the media over the years.

2. Claims and Counterclaims

As with any tragedy involving human lives and injuries, claims and counterclaims persisted at the time and have continued through the years. Numerous individuals over the decades have claimed to be (a)the first person on the scene of the disaster; (b)the last living survivor of the disaster. One particular claim was that of Harry Ellsworth Bennett. In a newspaper clipping dated October 23, 1941, from the file of the Ohio Room of the Ashtabula Public Library, Bennett claimed to be 101 years old, and to have been a survivor of the accident, upon the occasion of a brief visit to Ashtabula, stating that he was the news seller on the train that fateful night, December 29, 1876. He said he was one of the thirty-five survivors of the wreck, and that he spent eleven months in the hospital with an injured eye and back. Bennett made his claim, though it does not appear to withstand close scrutiny. If Bennett had been truthful about his age, he would have been thirty-six years of age at the time of the Ashtabula bridge disaster, a fairly mature age for a job that was traditionally reserved for a boy. The Coroner's Jury and several newspapers made reference to "the newsboy," which would not seem appropriate for one who was as old as the locomotive engineer and almost twice the age of the locomotive's fireman.

Lists of the dead and wounded do not bear the name of Bennett, though Bennett claimed to have been severely injured and to have lost an eye in the conflagration. If, as he claimed in 1941, Bennett had spent eleven months in the hospital, it seems likely that his name would have been noted. The one person identified as "newsboy" in all the lists was one George Covey of Buffalo, New York. The 1941 article stated that it was Bennett's first visit to Ashtabula "since he left the Ashtabula hospital sixty-four years ago." Of course, there was no Ashtabula hospital at the time of the train-bridge disaster, a key factor that rallied the community to establish a hospital.

Bennett also asserted that he had been the beneficiary of a settlement with the railroad that provided one dollar per day for as long as he lived. He opined that the railroad did not think he would live long and reached such a settlement in the expectation that it would cost the railroad little. To the point in 1941, he had collected over twenty-four thousand dollars. But elsewhere, the railroad claimed that the total cost of all settlements for the Ashtabula disaster was $458,422, including a high of $13,100 and a lowest settlement of $36. When he visited Ashtabula in 1941, Mr. Bennett appeared to be in a hurry and refused to discuss details of the disaster. By comparison, the newspaper reported the settlement the Lake Shore Railway managers reached with D. H. Clark of Westfield, Mass. "They allowed him two hundred dollars a month for three months' lost time, the value of his stock of goods, tools, clothing, etc., destroyed, besides doctor's bills, and bonus enough to swell the amount to sixteen hundred dollars" (*Ashtabula Sentinel,* March, 1877).

3. The Interim without a Bridge and the Building of the New Bridge

For all that has been written about the bridge disaster, little attention has been directed to the temporary efforts required during the time the bridge was out of commission or to the replacement structure. The first newspaper after the wreck announced that a Howe truss bridge, 160-feet long, at Case Avenue in Cleveland was being removed to Ashtabula to be cut to the correct length. It stated that the replacement bridge would be in service the following Thursday, January 11. A construction train had arrived on the Ashtabula scene Saturday afternoon, following the Friday night tragedy (*Ashtabula News,* January 3, 1877). Soon after the disaster, Mr. Collins placed the cost of the lost bridge at seventy thousand dollars. He was then quoted in the *Ashtabula Sentinel* (January 4, 1877) as saying that "it will not take much less than ten days to build a temporary bridge so that trains can cross." He estimated it would take two days to remove bodies and debris. In the meantime, he projected bringing together workers from Jamestown, Port Clinton, Sandusky, and other places. He planned to take "the old wooden bridge used the previous year at the Wilson Avenue crossing in Cleveland," which was the proper length, and which was at Collinwood. He said it could be brought to Ashtabula and erected "as fast as the weather will permit." It was January 17 before the replacement bridge was in service.

First over the new bridge was the locomotive Rambler, running to Kingsville to clear the snow and ice from the track. Then, drawn by two locomotives, the Dauntless and Mentor, passenger train No. 6, with three coaches and the usual number of baggage and express cars, left the depot with Chief Engineer Charles Collins and other Lake Shore officials on board. The *Ashtabula Sentinel* noted that "When the train reached the bridge the train was moving as rapidly as the two locomotives could draw it and passed over the bridge with scarcely a perceptible jar, the people on the cars and on the bridge cheering, and waving their hats and handkerchiefs" (January 18, 1877).

As early as January 3, 1877, three days after the wreck, the newspaper noted that "a large number of transfers was made each way" and "the transferring will continue until the bridge is rebuilt." The newspaper reported that "On Monday men were sent to build shanties on the east side for the protection of passengers awaiting transfer" (*Ashtabula News*, January 3, 1877).

Work had already begun on the framework for the new bridge, and "until a new structure is completed the transfer of passengers and baggage will be effected by teams over a mile and one-half of road." Later, the *Sentinel* reported that "passengers and baggage are transferred from one side of the gap to the other in sleighs" (*Ashtabula Sentinel*, January 4 and January 11, 1877).

4. Unusual Materials Salvaged from the Wreckage

With one estimate that there may have been a total of three tons of mail on the train (*Ashtabula News*, January 3, 1877), some half dozen sacks of mail matter, according to the *Ashtabula Sentinel* for June 11, 1877, were taken from the wreck to the post office. "Badly soaked as well as badly burned," the letters and papers still bore mostly legible addresses and seemed to be mostly for the far West and California. They were spread and dried and forwarded. Among "express matter" on the wrecked train were about seven cases (two dozen copies each) of *Bradstreet's Commercial Reports*. Only about one dozen were saved (*Ashtabula News*, January 10, 1877).

Four or five thousand dollars' worth of stamped bank checks, destined mostly for Texas banks, were salvaged. Though in damaged condition, all were thought to be redeemable. A box of kid gloves worth about twelve hundred dollars was badly burned but recovered. A box containing a bushel or more of pocketknives was broken open by the fall, and scattered in the water, from whence most were recollected (*Ashtabula News*, January 10, 1877). The train's two express safes were found in the water, their contents wet, but recovered (*Ashtabula News*, January 3, 1877).

A coat belonging to one of the deceased, Mr. George A. Purington, an express agent from Buffalo, was found and in the pocket was an accident policy for two thousand dollars.

A large handful of rings was gathered over the time of the cleanup, "with not a letter or word on one of them to reveal their owners" (*Ashtabula News*, January 10, 1877).

Eventually, Mr. E. W. Richards, the coroner, kept in his office and in a room rented for the purpose, a collection of the relics of the bridge disaster, "all damaged by fire and most utterly worthless." The relics included: fragments of clothing, jewelry, books, pocketknives, etc., and it was the judgment of the newspaper that they could easily be identified by the proper authorities (presumably, family or friends). Richards was to keep them through the year and then offer them for sale (*Ashtabula News*, April 18, 1877).

5. Removing the Debris and the Engine Columbia

The iron scraps of the bridge were carefully examined as they were removed from the crash site. The iron was hauled up the hill on sleds and loaded onto railcars, with every piece of metal being carefully measured and noted as to any breaks.

About January 18, the new bridge in service, a first attempt was made to bring the Columbia up from the gulf but failed (*Ashtabula Telegraph,* January 26, 1877). However, in dislodging the big engine from its resting place since the night of the disaster, they found silver coins, watches, and other property. Later, on approximately January 24, the Columbia was placed on a track up a very steep bank, and two engines hitched to it by means of iron rods and heavy ropes. When the wreck had nearly reached the top, one of the iron rods broke, sending the engine back down into the valley. The newspaper reported, "Being very heavy, and having a run of at least 100 feet, it plunged into the earth about ten feet, almost burying itself" (*Ashtabula Sentinel,* January 25, 1877). But the next day the engine was "drawn up, placed upon the track, and run off for repairs" (*Ashtabula Telegraph,* January 26, 1877).

6. Reports of Thievery

Reports of thievery were filed almost immediately, and the Mayor's quick action in posting guards over the site, appears to support the vulnerability of the disaster scene to plunder.

Sunday, December 31, less than two full days after the accident, all the wounded who had been left at Mulligan's were taken away to better quarters. The *Ashtabula News* (January 3, 1877) reported that some of those temporarily housed at Mulligan's "said they had been robbed of money and other valuables since the accident." The *Ashtabula Sentinel* (January 11, 1877) later claimed that "experienced robbers" were on the scene.

Thursday, January 4, Mayor Hepburn, having heard firsthand of the complaints of thievery, issued a proclamation notifying all parties having in their possession articles taken from the wreck, or otherwise not their own property, to turn such property over at once to the proper authorities. A considerable amount of goods was turned in, including a diamond ring with an original value of $500, but with the damage of fire and heat, its value was probably about $160. Two shawls, a pair of shoes, a pair of overshoes, and a pair of gloves were also turned in.

The *Ashtabula News* (January 17, 1877) noted that James Good was arrested for theft related to the accident and victims. James Porter was also arrested after goods were found on his premises. Porter was tried before the Mayor and bound over in the sum of one hundred dollars. Porter testified before the Coroner's Jury, January 2, and was one of the earliest persons on the scene. He was responsible for a restaurant at the west end of the Culver House, a hotel at the depot. Three other cases were at the time waiting to be tried, while several persons were let go, after they returned goods taken, and paid a small fine. The services of the sheriff and special detectives were employed. At least one New York detective was on hand, seeking to trace valuables, though who retained him was not clear.

E. A. Hitchcock, a member of the Ashtabula Village Council, and a local manufacturer, testified that on the night of the accident, he "saw people overhauling what I supposed was the express matter." "I know some things were thrown up; and I spoke about somebody's being put in charge, as there was no one there to take charge." He encountered Mr. Strong, the local station master, and "spoke to him about that express matter being overhauled as it was. He said he would go down then, or send down, and attend to it" (*Ashtabula News*, January 17, 1877).

In a compassionate letter to Mr. Brunner, whose son,

daughter-in-law, and two grandchildren were lost in the accident, Acting Coroner E. W. Richards stated: "There has never been a doubt in my mind that there was some fearful plundering done during the first confusion and before a regular watch was set over everything." (Richards to Samuel Brunner, October 29, 1877).

7. The Curiosity of the Train-Bridge Accident

Almost immediately, curiosity about the Ashtabula train-bridge accident was overwhelming. "At the earliest hour on Saturday morning our citizens began to gather at the scene of the catastrophe, remaining in large numbers during the day," stated the *Ashtabula News* (January 3, 1877). Sunday following the crash, "hosts of people" came to Ashtabula by railroad and other means "so that the part of town near the scene of the accident was thronged. Hotels and boarding houses have been taxed to their utmost capacities by the numbers of guests, friends of the sufferers, and others" (*Ashtabula News,* January 3, 1877).

The telegraph office was strained to capacity, and crowds seemed to have kept coming throughout the first week or two. An article in the *Ashtabula Sentinel* for January 11, 1887, states that day (the 11th) was "the first day that has not witnessed more or less of a crowd of interested spectators at the west abutment of the bridge."

At last, by April 18, 1877, editors of the *Ashtabula News* took a philosophical view.

> Not many traces yet remain at the scene of the great railroad accident. A few piles of burned debris, and the blackened appearance of the abutment are about all that would now be noticed, and soon even those will disappear in the verdure of Spring. Even so soon, too, do the memories of that awful night and following day begin to seem almost like a vivid and terrible dream; for thus to our minds, as in the visible world does nature ever hide the faces of death, and life springs ever from decay.

Of course, the accident occupied the attention of the public for many years afterward, and curiosity seekers would have continued to explore, even as family and friends treated the site with special significance. One story has it that about twenty years after the accident, a man disembarked from an inbound train at the New York Central depot and asked a bystander for directions to the site of the Ashtabula disaster. It happened that the bystander was a reporter for the *Ashtabula Daily Beacon,* and he accompanied the stranger to the scene, discovering on the way that the stranger was Ira D. Sankey, noted evangelist, who had worked with D. L. Moody, and who was a close friend and collaborator of P. P. Bliss. The reporter commented that Sankey was "deeply moved" as he looked over the valley where his friend was killed.

Hundreds of travelers, in the years following the accident, must have had an experience somewhat like that of Henry Drummond (1851–1897), Scottish science professor, later to become famous as the writer of the devotional classic, *The Greatest Thing in the World.* Drummond visited the United States in 1879, just two-and-a-half years after the Ashtabula disaster, as part of a geological expedition. While most of his visit was in the West, especially the Rocky Mountains, he concluded his American trip with a few days in Boston. There, he declined dinner with Henry Wadsworth Longfellow and Oliver Wendell Holmes, in order to take the train to Cleveland where evangelist D. L. Moody and Ira D. Sankey, whom he had known during their first visit to England when he was a university student, were holding special meetings. Drummond told this story of his train ride.

> Some fifty miles, perhaps—before reaching the city [Cleveland], the train slowed somewhat, and I observed two gentlemen in the next compartment look with a sudden interest out of the window at the left. I followed

their example instinctively, and found that we were rolling along a high viaduct which spanned a dark ravine. At one end lay a small pile of newly dressed stones, as if the bridge had been recently repaired. The thought seized me somehow that I knew this place, that I had seen it in words or a picture at some former period. And then the impression came with the speed of lightning, and I found myself saying, Yes, this is it—the fatal bridge—the spot where P. P. Bliss was translated into a chariot of fire. I had not the most remote idea that among the tens of thousands of miles of railroad on that vast continent, I was traveling over the particular spot which embalms that tragic memory. . . . I learned from Mr. Sankey without any surprise, some hours later, of its correctness. The place was Ashtabula. (Henry Drummond, "A Visit to Mr. Moody and Mr. Sankey," *New Zealand Christian Record,* 1880.)

8. Settlements with the Railroad Company

To its credit, the Lake Shore and Michigan Southern Railway appeared eager to make financial settlements with victims and their families. A few of the settlements were reported in the public press and are summarized.

D. H. Clark, injured, $1500, representing his time for three months at $200 per month, his doctor's bills, and the value of his baggage

L. C. Crain, deceased, $5,175

D. M. Holdridge, deceased, $4,000

George Kepler, deceased, $5,000

Maggie L. Lewis, deceased, $3,000, plus $200 for incidental expenses

Peter Livenbroe, deceased, $3,000

Albert H. Stockwell, deceased, offer of $5,000

Unidentified widow was reported as having received $5,000, "as her right," and an additional $2500 as a gift from the company

While the newspapers could be critical of the railroad, it

commended the company for the promptness and quality of the settlements. As reported in the *Telegraph*, February 23, 1877, "The readiness with which these arrangements are entered into by the L. S. Company [sic] cannot be viewed in any other light than as generous and honorable."

The *News*, of February 28, 1877, quoted the *St. Louis Globe–Democrat*, reporting that the railroad had settled with sixty of the sufferers, and "in every instance in a satisfactory manner. This action speaks well for the officers of the road."

9. Heroines and Heroes

In such a tragic event, it is to be expected that certain individuals might have rendered uncommon service. Most names cannot be known, and we are left only to appreciate the courtesy and kindness of the majority of citizens of the village when the terrible tragedy was visited upon them. From the perspective of today, the identities of only a few are apparent; since the names are not well-known to history, it seems appropriate to mention a few who seem to have demonstrated exceptional courage and/or compassion in the Ashtabula railway-bridge disaster.

Marion Shepard, of Beloit, Wisconsin, was compared to an "angel." As a passenger, she rescued herself with some assistance, and then stayed close to the wreckage through the fire, helping people, consoling them, and even comforting the mortally wounded. Her story is chronicled more completely in Appendix A and in the text of the essays.

Sophie Farrington was mentioned by a Kingsville writer in "high terms and admiration of the humanity and energy in looking after and making provision for the wounded and suffering, and [the writer] jocosely remarks that had she been at the head of the fire department, water would have been used for putting out the fires of the burning wreck" (*Sentinel*, January 11, 1877).

E. W. Richards was asked to serve as acting coroner, when the elected coroner failed to qualify. Richards, a justice of the peace, brought orderly administration to the chaos of the accident, the inventorying of relics, salvaged personal effects, bodies and body parts. He appears to have accounted for every item. He coordinated the visits of family and friends to the temporary morgue, and corresponded compassionately with families and inquirers. At the same time, he was dealing with the Coroner's Jury and its inquest. He managed an enormous responsibility with apparent civility and kindness.

L. B. Sturges, of St. Paul, MN, got out of the last sleeper car with only scratches and bruises, but he helped two or three others get out of the wreck, including a large man with a broken leg, who was difficult to extricate through the window.

Charles Tooley, of Ashtabula, rescued a little girl from a burning railcar and brought her up the steep bank unaided (*News,* January 3, 1877).

The kindness of many Ashtabula residents providing housing and hospitality for the injured is most impressive. Some injured were required to stay eight or ten weeks. Even the relatives coming to claim remains, and to look for personal effects were often accommodated in the homes of local citizens. Local doctors were also responsive. According to the newspapers, some who provided housing were identified, along with some attending physicians.

Mr. Baker housed Alexander Monroe, of Somerville, MA, until mid-February.

Dr. Bartlett, physician, cared for Edward Truworthy of Oakland, CA; and Joseph A. Thompson, of Oakland, CA.

Mrs. Sanborn housed A. E. Hewitt of Bridgeport, CT, until mid-February.

M. H. Haskell housed Henry W. Shepard of Brooklyn, NY until mid-February.

Mayor H. P. Hepburn housed Henry T. Tomlinson until mid-February, and then had his funeral at the Hepburn home. Later, the Mayor accompanied Mrs. Tomlinson back to Bridgeport, CT with the body of her husband.

Dr. Hubbard, physician, cared for Alfred H. Parslow of Chicago;

Dr. A. L. King, physician, cared for A. E. Hewitt, of Bridgeport, CT; Thomas J. Jackson, of Waterbury, CT; F. A. Ormsbee, of Boston. A letter to the newspaper from Mr. Hewitt, after he had arrived at his home, complimented the city of Ashtabula on having such a fine person as Dr. King as a physician.

Mrs. Nelson housed Frank L. Collier, of Elmira, NY, until the end of February.

Dr. Wallace housed Alfred H. Parslow, of Chicago, until late January.

10. "Relics"

Somehow, the term ascribed to everything remaining after the accident was "relic." It was used to describe personal effects and possessions, as well as debris from the train. As author David Tobias describes in his essay, he is still finding items from the train accident, more than 125 years later. It is likely that some items, salvaged from the wreckage, still make the rounds of local antique shops. In 2003, it was possible to buy old items marked "LS&MS," though it would be difficult to prove they came from the accident of 1876.

Aside from the relics, and the two lithographs reproduced elsewhere in this volume, the only known contemporary attempt at creating a souvenir or memento of the Ashtabula train-bridge accident was that of A. M. Smith. As reported in the *Cleveland Herald,* and reproduced in the *Ashtabula News,* February 28, 1877:

A. M. Smith, of Ashtabula, has had manufactured a number of canes made from the wood of the car Palatine, which went down in that fearful December disaster. He offers them for sale to those whose strange taste craves an ornamental memento of the awful occurrence.

On February 9, 1877, the *Jefferson Gazette* carried this item, later reproduced in the *Ashtabula News* of February 14, 1877:

If you have not got a cane made from the Ashtabula wreck you are not in fashion.

APPENDIX F

PROGRAM

Bliss and Tragedy: A 125ᵗʰ Year Remembrance of Songwriter Philip Paul Bliss and the Ashtabula Bridge Disaster
December 29, 1876 — August 2-4, 2002
Ashtabula, Ohio

Steering Committee
    The Reverend Virgil Reeve, Coordinator
    Neil Crislip, Finance Secretary
    Monica M. Rocco, Treasurer
    The Reverend Neroy Carter
    Paula DeMichele
    The Reverend John M. Germaine
    Barbara J. Hamilton
    Darrell E. Hamilton
    The Reverend Michael Legg
    The Reverend Dr. Stephen Long
    Hector Martinez
    Gerald Thurston
    The Reverend Donis Williams
    Joe Cook (Honorary)
    Dr. Thomas E. Corts, Guest Chair

Friday Evening
August 2, 2002 — Seven O'Clock

Piano Prelude of Bliss Songs
Stan Whitmire, Pianist

Invocation
The Reverend Neroy Carter

Welcome
Susan Stocker

Welcome and Presentation of Keys to the City
The Honorable August Pugliese, City Manager of Ashtabula

"Bliss. . .Still A Blessing"
Dr. Thomas E. Corts

Unveiling
"Bird's Eye View of the Ashtabula Horror"
An original charcoal drawing by Mervin Clary

Bliss Songs — Sing-a-Long
Frank Boggs and the Congregation

Bliss and Tragedy

Bliss Anecdotes
Dr. Thomas E. Corts

"It Is Well with My Soul"
(Arranged by Mary McDonald)
Messiah Lutheran Church Choir\Directed by Ruth Ann Martinez

Bliss Selections
Frank Boggs

Benediction
The Reverend Dr. Stephen R. Long

Saturday Morning
August 3, 2002

10 a.m. "The Ashtabula Bridge Disaster from the Perspective of 125 Years"
Presiding, Paula DeMichele

Welcome to Ashtabula Township Cedarquist Park
Township Park Commissioners

Introduction to the Topic
Dr. Thomas E. Corts, Moderator

Panel Presentation and Discussion
Charles A. Burnham
Barbara J. Hamilton
Darrell E. Hamilton
John Paul
David G. Tobias

11.30 a.m. Bridge Disaster Site Visit – Meet at Cedarquist Park
Led by Charles A. Burnham and David G. Tobias
OR
11:15 a.m. Slide Show, Video Presentation, Artifacts Displays

Saturday Afternoon
August 3, 2002 — Two-Thirty O'Clock
Memorial Service
First United Methodist Church

Organ Prelude of Bliss Hymns

Welcome
The Reverend John M. Germaine

Call to Worship

Congregational Song No. 600 — "Wonderful Words of Life"

Old Testament Scripture — Jeremiah 6:10; Ezekiel 33:4–6
The Reverend Dr. Stephen R. Long

Historical Observations
The Reverend Barbara Johnson

Choir and Congregation — "There's a Light in the Valley"
(Arranged by Gene Milford for this occasion)

New Testament Scripture — Matthew 24:37–39, 44
The Reverend Michael Legg

Congregational Song No. 165 — "Hallelujah, What a Savior"

Prayer Remembering the Victims Who Died in the Valley 125 Years Ago
The Reverend Neroy Carter

Anthem — "It Is Well with My Soul"

Memorial Message
"Therefore Be Ye Also Ready" Matthew 24:44
The Reverend Virgil Reeve
Excerpts of the Sermon on the Death of P. P. Bliss by D. L. Moody
(Preached December 31, 1876 — two days after Bliss's tragic death)

Benediction
The Reverend John M. Germaine

3:30 Visit Monument to the Unrecognized Dead of the Ashtabula Bridge Disaster
Procession led by Ducro Horse-Drawn Funeral Hearse,
Color Guard Groups, Ashtabula Fire Department
Chestnut Grove Cemetery

Tolling of the Original Fire Station Bell 125 Times While En Route

Reading of Names of Crash Victims

"It Is Well with My Soul"
Trumpet Trio — Bill Ashbrook, Shelley Meister and Hector Martinez

"The Lord's Prayer"
Led by All Pastors Present

"Taps"
Trumpet Trio

Saturday Evening
August 3, 2002 — Seven O'Clock
Kent State University — Ashtabula Campus Auditorium

Presiding
The Reverend Virgil Reeve

Piano Prelude of Bliss Hymns
Stan Whitmire, Pianist

Invocation
The Reverend Donis Williams

"Bliss and Gospel Music in Our Culture"
Bliss Medley — Mae Salters, Soloist
Dr. Timothy Kalil, Pianist

167

Bliss and Tragedy

"A Bliss-fest of Gospel Songs"
Frank Boggs and Congregation

Bliss Anecdotes
Dr. Thomas E. Corts

Benediction
The Reverend John M. Germaine

Sunday Afternoon
August 4, 2002 — Four O'Clock
Kent State University — Ashtabula Campus — Outdoor Pavilion

Presiding
The Reverend Neroy Carter

Piano Prelude of Bliss Songs
Stan Whitmire, Pianist

Invocation
The Reverend Michael Legg

Instrumental Ensemble of Bliss Hymns
Led by Hector Martinez

Congregational Singing
Led by Frank Boggs
Stan Whitmire, Pianist

"Dare To Be A Daniel"
Children's Choir, Jesus Only Pentecostal Church
Directed by Nadena Carter

"Stories Behind Bliss Gospel Songs"
Dr. Thomas E. Corts

Volunteer Choir
Directed by Frank Boggs

"More Holiness Give Me"
Hector Martinez, Trumpet Soloist

Litany to Mark the 125th Anniversary of The Ashtabula Bridge Disaster

Closing Remarks
Dr. Thomas E. Corts

"It Is Well with My Soul"
Volunteer Choir Finale

Benediction
The Reverend Gary Warinner

APPENDIX G

A Timeline of the Life of Philip Paul Bliss
Adapted and abridged from research
by Anne Trousdale Gardner
(Some dates are approximate.)

1635   George Bliss (1591–1667) comes from England to Massachusetts; eventually settles in Newport, RI, in 1649.

1666   George's son, Major John Bliss, marries Demaris Arnold.

1685   John's son, Josiah Bliss, is born (1685–1748), becomes a member of the Seventh Day Baptist Church.

1728   Josiah's son, The Reverend William Bliss, is born (1728–1808), becomes a Seventh Day Baptist clergyman.

1760   William's son, John Bliss, is born (1760–1845), becomes a Revolutionary War veteran.

1787   John moves to Cambridge, Washington County, NY, where he lives for about four years before moving to Greenfield, Saratoga County, NY.

1797   John's twin sons, Isaac and Josiah, are born. John and wife, Reliance Babcock, have sixteen children, including twelve sons; at least ten of the children die before reaching maturity.

1801   John walks from Greenfield, NY to Newport, RI, to be baptized at the Seventh Day Baptist Church.

1807   John and wife, Reliance, are admitted into membership of the Berlin Seventh Day Baptist Church in Rensselaer County, NY; John is subsequently ordained as an evangelist despite a limited education.

1818   John sells his farm in Saratoga County; moves to Clearfield County, PA, where he builds a gristmill.

1831   June 7, Isaac Bliss marries Lydia Doolittle.

1832   May 27, Phebe Bliss is born.

1834 May 14, Reliance Bliss is born.

1838 July 9, Philip Paul Bliss is born near (two miles north) Penfield, Clearfield County, PA.

1842 May 1, Mary Elizabeth Bliss is born.

1844 Philip (age six) and the Bliss Family move to Kinsman in Trumbull County, OH.

1845 Philip starts making his own musical instruments.

1846 July 10, James Bliss is born.

1847 February 15, James Bliss dies; November 4, Reliance Bliss dies; Isaac Bliss and family move to Espyville, Crawford County, PA, near the Ohio border.

1848 Isaac Bliss with Philip (age ten) and his family move to Cherry Flats, Tioga County, PA, in north central Pennsylvania, near the New York border.

1849 Bliss (subsequent references are to Philip Paul Bliss) hears a piano for the first time.

1849 Bliss leaves home (age 11) to work on a neighbor's farm.

1850 Bliss (age 12) makes a public profession of faith at a Baptist revival meeting; later, he is baptized in a creek near his home.

1851 Bliss (age 13) works on a farm for nine dollars per month.

1852 Bliss (age 14) works as an assistant cook in a lumber camp in Pine Creek, PA; attends school as possible.

1855 At age 17, Bliss traveled 100 miles west to Bradford City, PA, to complete requirements for teaching credentials.

1856 Bliss (age 18) teaches school in Hartsville, Allegheny County, NY.

1857 Bliss (age 19) enters Susquehanna Collegiate Institute, Towanda, Bradford County, PA; Bliss meets William B. Bradbury at Musical Convention in Rome, Bradford County, PA; teaches at the school house on Towner Hill in Rome Township.

1858 Bliss (age 20) teaches at Rome Academy, Rome, PA; he and his sister, Mary Elizabeth, board with the Oscar F. and Rachel (Allen) Young family in Rome.

1859 June 1, Philip Bliss (age 21) marries Lucy Jane Young in parlor of the Presbyterian minister's home, Wysox, PA; Philip and Lucy join the Rome Presbyterian Church.

1860   Bliss attends music classes at Normal Academy of Music, Geneseo, NY, during the summer.
1861   March 4, Mary Elizabeth Bliss marries Clark Willson in Steuben County, NY.
1861–62 and '63 Bliss attends Normal Academy of Music in Geneseo; continues to conduct Singing Schools and Musical Conventions alone and with the Towners in Northeastern Pennsylvania and adjacent New York.
1863   Bliss (age 25) buys residence in Rome for his parents.
1864   Isaac Bliss dies; Lydia Bliss moves to Towanda to live with daughter, Mary E. Willson; Bliss's "Lora Vale" is published by George Frederick Root; Bliss (age 27) receives the flute he has requested as payment.
1865   Bliss is drafted into the military but is discharged within two weeks; "Yankee Boys" quartet, including Bliss, goes to Chicago to work with Root, the music publisher.
1869   Philip and Lucy Bliss celebrate tenth wedding anniversary; first meet evangelist D. L. Moody on Chicago street corner.
1870   Fall, Philip Bliss (age 32) has first meeting with Ira Sankey in Chicago; Sankey becomes familiar with Bliss's songs; Bliss becomes musical director/choirmaster of First Congregational Church, Chicago; many Bliss songs are included in *The Prize*, Bliss's music book for children; "Hold the Fort!;" "I Am So Glad That Jesus Loves Me."
1871   Bliss (age 33) compiles *The Charm*, a music book for Sunday Schools; "Almost Persuaded," "Let the Lower Lights Be Burning," "There's A Light in the Valley;" October 7 & 8, the Great Chicago Fire destroys the Bliss's (age 33) home, and place of employment, The Publishing House of Root and Cady.
1872   Paul Bliss is the first child born to Lucy and Philip Paul Bliss (age 34) in Chicago; songbook, *The Song Tree*, is published.
1873   Bliss (age 35) compiles *The Sunshine* for Sunday schools and *The Joy* for choirs and musical conventions; "Dare To Be a Daniel," "Free from the Law," "More Holiness Give Me," "I Gave My Life for Thee"

1873–74 From Scotland, Moody urges Bliss to become full-time evangelistic singer-songleader.

1874   Bliss and D. W. Whittle consecrate their lives to setting forth the Gospel in word and song; Bliss publishes *Gospel Songs;* "Wonderful Words of Life," "Precious Promise," "Hallelujah! 'Tis Done;"August 27, George Goodwin Bliss (second son of Philip and Lucy) is born in Chicago, IL.

1875   Bliss, with Ira Sankey, publishes *Gospel Hymns and Sacred Songs,* both an edition with music and a words-only edition.

1876   "It Is Well with My Soul" matches Bliss's music to the words of Horatio Spafford; the Blisses work with Whittle throughout the South, at Chautauqua, and elsewhere; December 29, 1876 Philip and Lucy Bliss are killed in the Ashtabula railway-bridge disaster.

1877   January 7, memorial services are held at Rome Presbyterian Church, Rome, PA, for the Blisses; memorial services also held in many other cities; *Gospel Hymns #2* is published ten days after the Blisses' deaths; Lucy's youngest sister, Clara, and her husband, John Ellsworth, agree to raise the two Bliss sons, Paul and George, with their own son, Charles; January 19, memorial services held in Ashtabula, Ohio; July 10, cenotaph is dedicated in Rome (PA) cemetery.

1933   Paul Bliss dies, February 2, in Owego, NY; George Bliss dies, December 29, same day (not same year) as his parents, in Candor, NY; each was survived by his wife, though neither had children.

Appendix H
The Fire and Water Controversy

The most controversial aspect of the Ashtabula bridge disaster, by all accounts, was the failure to put out the fire. Candles for light and coal stoves for heat, both common on trains of that day, provided plenty of ignition. The fall and crash landing of railcars upon railcars scattered the flames from the candles and stoves in all directions. From the testimony of survivors, we know that stoves ricocheted around the cars as they fell and crashed, crushing people in their paths and spewing flames with force. The great amount of well-varnished woodwork and lumber superstructure of the railcars provided ample fuel. A great heaping bonfire was the result.

From the moment the tragedy befell the city, it was unclear as to who should be in charge. Individuals in the employ of the Lake Shore and Michigan Southern Railway (LS&MS) obviously had a vested interest. It could be argued that even the rail employees had no understanding of a chain of command: i.e., who among all the railroad workers present was the ranking authority? No executive or crisis management personnel were on the scene. Word of the wreck had been telegraphed almost immediately up and down the line, lest other trains should come from either direction and happen onto the suddenly bridge-less chasm, unaware. Key among local personnel would have been the station agent, A. A. Strong, whose duties normally related to the operation of the station as a whole. The only official word, according to Mr. Charles Philbrook, a resident of Painesville and a thirty-three-year-old painter in charge of the painting division of the railroad, came while he was supervising some lettering being done when the accident happened, and he went to help. Philbrook said that he was told he had the only message anyone had received from the railroad. It was sent to Mr. Strong, but

Philbrook was unable to find Strong. The message read:

> Cleveland, Dec. 29th. Send uptown and get all the surgeons and
> help that you can. Do all you can for the passengers call all the
> help you can. [signed] C.B.C. [1]

The only other message that night from officials of the railroad,
appears to have been a message addressed to Mr. Henn, the
conductor, and it read:

> Get the number of wounded, and send to me. [2]

Therefore, news of the tragedy spread slowly among rail
authorities, although the magnitude and specific details of the
crisis were probably not widely known.

Other employees on duty that night might have included a
baggagemaster, responsible for baggage and passengers
claiming and managing their personal luggage; an express
manager, who would normally see to packages and freight that
were unaccompanied by any passenger. The surviving engineer
and conductor would be expected to also have some degree of
authority in the situation.

The village had a responsibility for the safety of its citizens,
and its mayor might have been expected to assume leadership.
To some extent, Mayor H. P. Hepburn may have been
compromised by also being an employee of the LS&MS Railway,
but he was on the scene and was certainly not aloof or
uninvolved. In testimony afterward, the Mayor indicated that he
was at the site within thirty minutes of the initial accident, but
that to put water on the fire at that point would have scalded
survivors. After the event, the Mayor was charged with having
given the order not to apply water. The Mayor got Chief Knapp
to issue a signed statement to the Coroner's Jury stating that the

---

1 *Ashtabula News,* January 10, 1877.

2 Ibid.

Mayor had not given such an order, nor had the Mayor and the Chief had conversation on that subject on the night of the tragedy. But the *Ashtabula Telegraph* (January 5, 1877) still wondered: "Would it not be gratifying to the public to know from the Mayor and Chief, their reasons for not using the facilities at hand for quenching the fire?"

It might be expected that the fire chief would be in charge. G. A. Knapp, the chief of firemen, testified that "he supposed that no one had any right to give him orders in such a time, and that his authority was supreme" (testimony before the Coroner's Jury, *Ashtabula Sentinel*, January 11, 1877). Yet, his inaction is a matter of record.

From the time of the accident until fire companies were there was about twenty minutes, according to Peet.[3] At least one fire engine was in the engine house at the Lake Avenue station, near the track.

What seems to have happened was a massive exercise in noncommunication. Without there being any clear authority in charge, the following sequence of events appears to have happened:

- Mr. A. A. Strong, the station agent, was present almost immediately and asked Mr. Apthorp, an employee of the Railroad, what should be done. Apthorp answered, "Get men to help up the wounded."

- The chief fireman, Mr. Knapp, arrived and asked Mr. Strong where to put the hose, where to put the water? The only response was an echo of Mr. Apthorp, "We want to get out the wounded, never mind the water." A second time the question was asked of the station agent, in another place, and the response was, "We don't want water, we want to get out the wounded."

- As firemen laid out their hose, again the statement was made that there was no use throwing water on the flames.

- As Peet so delicately states it, "The chief fireman was not

---

3 Stephen D. Peet, *The Ashtabula Disaster* (Chicago, 1877).

a man to assume the responsibility under such circumstances: he was dazed and confused and did not seem to know what to do." [4]

- A call went out for buckets, and from somewhere new buckets appeared. Men took buckets and went into the mass of wreckage seeking to rescue bodies from the burning. Gradually, and without direct orders, firemen took up the pails and went to work on the fire, there being no other orders given.

- The driver took the steamer, drove it to the cistern, and stationed it there. The whistle of the steamer was sounded for hose, and men stood readily by. No orders came.

- The captain of the steamer asked the station agent if he should apply water, but the same answer was returned.

- The chief fireman still "remained stupid and passive, and gave no orders." [5]

- A few considered taking the hand-pump engine down the embankment to the creek. Though arrangements were made, and the hose was attached, the foreman decided against it. Later, in testimony before the Coroner's Jury, Chief Knapp testified that the only order he gave was to Mr. Drake, foreman of the Protection Company, whom he instructed to convey his engine to the flats, but the foreman did not obey (reported in *Ashtabula Sentinel,* January 11, 1877).

Peet concluded:

The strangest misunderstanding has taken possession of all. Whatsoever the motive of those in authority, the effect was, to keep the engines from playing upon the flames. There were tanks on both sides of the track; the engines were both on the ground; there was hose sufficient, but the misunderstanding made everything useless, and the department was held back and did nothing (p. 54).

Afterward, much discussion centered around whether anyone realized that the hoses of the Lake Erie engine and

---

4 Peet, *The Ashtabula Disaster,* p. 50.

5 Ibid., p. 51.

engine house would fit the fireplug at the pump house, where no hose was routinely kept. While the priority response was to attempt to aid the wounded and help survivors to safety, amidst cries for help and people obviously battling for their lives, no clear, authoritative voice rang out with instructions concerning the fire or to fire personnel. For all those assembled, no such tragedy had ever been confronted previously. The fast-moving fire spread from west to east, and in only about thirty minutes' time, the fire was beyond recovery.

The *Ashtabula Sentinel* (January 4, 1877) editorialized:

> One story was that the firemen were forbidden to throw water on the burning wreck. The story, which if it is a fact is too monstrous to believe; but upon investigation it seems to dwindle away, and of all the evidence elicited from the coroners inquest, and the searching enquiries of the reporters, no one can trace it directly to the one who issued the order.

After the accident, Chief Knapp was first rumored to resign, but concluded not to do so. The *Ashtabula Telegraph* (February 9, 1877) then asked: "Will they now bounce him?" By the 28th of February, Knapp had resigned, and Mayor Hepburn had appointed H. H. Hill as chief (*Ashtabula News,* February 28, 1877).

Today, the antique fire bell, which once hung in the old Lake Street Fire Station in Ashtabula, rests in front of the Fire Station at 4326 Main Avenue. It is the very bell that sounded the alarm, the night of December 29, 1876. The bell was donated in 1975 by Mrs. Lena Fox Schlacter, in memory of Mr. and Mrs. John C. Poole, longtime residents of Ashtabula.

Appendix I
Information Discovered on Survivors
since First Printing

Johnson B. Orburn and wife
Mr. and Mrs. Orburn were inconsistently cited among contemporary rosters of the injured. However, the *Daily Inter-Ocean,* January 10, 1877, relates how Mr. Orburn was extricated from the wreckage of the Ashtabula bridge disaster, and how his wife's dress was aflame. Subsequently, the couple walked from the accident site to the hotel, "having escaped with only a few bruises." The newspaper identified the Orburns as "past 40, and Mr. Orburn as an Ohio farmer, who lately purchased a farm in Saginaw County [Michigan]."

——— **Hyderman, Albany, New York**
Mr. Hyderman's name does not appear on any contemporary roster of survivors. Yet, the *Ashtabula News,* of April 18, 1877, almost four months after the disaster, quotes a dispatch from Albany, New York, "of last Saturday," noting that "Mr. Hyderman, a tobacconist of this city, who was injured in the Ashtabula disaster, was taken sick yesterday, and died today." Apparently, his terminal illness was unrelated to injuries sustained in the Ashtabula accident.

Mrs. T. A. Davis, Kokomo, Indiana
The *Kokomo Weekly Dispatch,* for January 4, 1877, notes that Mrs. Davis returned home to Kokomo on Monday, January 1, 1877, following the accident. In the January 11, 1877 edition of the paper, it is noted that Mrs. Davis was among the first to escape from the wreckage with "only minor bruises."

Ellen Austin and Mary Austin, Omaha, Nebraska
Ellen and Mary were sisters and were presumed to have perished in the disaster. However, the *Daily Inter-Ocean,* for January 9, 1877, reported that the two sisters had been found alive and well in Buffalo, New York.

Libbee Myers, Buffalo, New York
The *Daily Inter-Ocean* for January 8, 1877, reported that Miss Myers' remains were positively identified by friends. With the unusual spelling of her forename, and the similarity of last handwritten names, it appears that "Libbie Negus" and Libbee Myers, cited in the *Daily Inter-Ocean* referenced above, are one and the same individual.

Contributors

Dr. Thomas E. Corts, Editor

Thomas E. Corts was born in Terre Haute, Indiana, in 1941. His family moved to Akron, Ohio, and then to Ashtabula, where he attended State Road School, Division Street School, Station Avenue School, and Park Junior High School, before graduation from Ashtabula High School in 1959. He earned a bachelor's degree at Georgetown College in Kentucky, and M.A. and Ph.D. degrees at Indiana University. In addition, he was awarded three honorary doctoral degrees. From 1983 to 2006, Corts was president of Samford University in Birmingham, Alabama, at that time a 4300-student institution, ranked by *U.S. News & World Report* among the top universities in the South. While Samford's president, he also served as president of the Southern Association of Colleges and Schools, president of the American Association of Presidents of Independent Colleges and Universities, and chairman of the President's Advisory Council of the Association of Governing Boards of Colleges and Universities. In July 2006, he was named president emeritus of Samford University. Shortly thereafter, he was appointed interim chancellor of the Alabama College System. A year later, he briefly served as the executive director of the International Association of Baptist Colleges and Universities before being appointed by the President of the United States to the position of coordinator for the President's International Education Initiative at the U. S. Agency for International Development. Dr. Corts died on February 4, 2009, and is survived by his wife, Marla Ruth Haas, of Ashtabula, his high school sweetheart. They have three children and eight grandchildren.

Charles A. Burnham is the founder of the Ashtabula Railway Historical Foundation (ARHF). Through the viewpoint of his engineering degree, he was fascinated with the causes of the bridge collapse and sought to share the results of his findings through the ARHF's web site. He has given tours of the disaster site, and works with local historical societies comparing notes and making corrections as needed. Each Memorial Day weekend, he supervises an ARHF group to plant flowers in memory of the unrecognized dead and fallen train crew at the monument in Chestnut Grove Cemetery and a historical monument near Ashtabula County Medical Center. Born in Ashtabula, he grew up in North Kingsville and graduated from Edgewood Senior High School in 1987. He received his bachelor's degree in engineering in 1992 from Bryant and Stratton College in Cleveland, OH. He currently is a research and development engineer for Nidec-Kinetek Controls in Perry, an eastern suburb of Cleveland, Ohio. He lives in Ashtabula, and has two daughters Cassandra and Caitlyn.

Barbara J. Hamilton is vice president of the Jefferson Historical Society of Jefferson, Ohio, and as such, has helped research, compile, and write county history with the help of her husband, Bill, a history buff too. She researched and authored the book, *Where Have All the Schoolhouses Gone?*, a history of the schools, teachers, and students in Ashtabula County, Ohio from 1854 to 1954. Her love of history spreads even further to a special interest in veterans of all wars. Barbara has interviewed several hundred veterans and writes their stories for publication in their local papers. For ten years, she has covered D-Day Conneaut, an annual reenactment of D-Day, held in Conneaut, Ohio. Barbara and Bill make their home in the Lenox Township area, where Bill's family runs Hamilton's Dairy. They are the parents of four grown children.

Darrell E. Hamilton graduated from Ashtabula High School in 1969, attended Kent State University—Ashtabula campus, and completed a bachelor's degree at Morehead State University, before doing further graduate study at Ohio State University. While researching the facts of the Ashtabula train disaster, he noted the national significance of the event since most of the survivors and victims were not from Ashtabula but from around the country— New York City, Cleveland, Chicago, Omaha, and Oakland, California.

Bliss and Tragedy

Timothy M. Kalil was an instructor of music at Kent State University—Ashtabula Campus. He grew up in Ashtabula, where the bridge disaster was a part of local history and lore that he heard discussed in his family's two businesses (founded in 1907 and in 1963) both located near the train depot area. He earned the Ph.D. degree at Kent State University where he specialized in musicology and ethnomusicology, with a dissertation on Thomas A. Dorsey, "The Father of Black Gospel Music."

David G. Tobias lives with his cat in Ashtabula within walking distance of the site of the disaster and waits patiently for his granddaughter to become old enough to visit the site. He grew up in Ashtabula and graduated from Edgewood High School. In the 1960s, he began roaming the site of the Ashtabula bridge disaster and found an old pocketknife. Later, he utilized a metal detector and gathered buckets of metal objects, railcar hardware, rail spikes, jewelry fragments, and coins. His impressive collection has grown rapidly. Some of his choice findings are pictured within this book, but only a portion. He says, "The lure, the thrill, and the satisfaction of gathering and preserving history has never departed." For many years, David has taken his vast collection of artifacts to show to school groups and historical societies. When younger, David placed muskrat traps along the Ashtabula River in the area of the two large arches that ultimately replaced the fallen Ashtabula bridge of 1876. Little did he realize he would become the best known collector of Ashtabula bridge disaster artifacts.

Index

Made in the USA
Middletown, DE
06 February 2015